# CHAMPION SPORT

## BIOGRAPHIES

# MARTINA HINGIS

# CHAMPION SPORT
## BIOGRAPHIES

# MARTINA HINGIS

**BEV SPENCER**

Warwick Publishing Inc.
Toronto Los Angeles
www.warwickgp.com

© 1999 Maverick Communications

We acknowledge the financial support of the Government of Canada through the Book Publishing Industry Development Program for our publishing activities.

ISBN: 1-894020-49-9

Published by Warwick Publishing Inc.
162 John Street, Suite 300, Toronto, Ontario, Canada M5V 2E5
1300 North Alexandria Avenue, Los Angeles, California 90027

Distributed in the United States and Canada by Firefly Books Ltd.
3680 Victoria Park Avenue, Willowdale, Ontario M2H 3K1

Cover and layout design: Heidi Gemmill
Editorial Services: Joseph Romain
Photos courtesy AP/Wide World Photos

Printed and bound in Canada.

# Table of Contents

Factsheet .......................................................................6

Introduction ................................................................7

Chapter 1 — Laying the Groundwork .....................13

Chapter 2 — The Power Behind the Star .................17

Chapter 3 — Tennis Close-Up: A Pro's Technique...22

Chapter 4 — Going Pro: A Controversial Move. ....33

Chapter 5 — A Star Rising: Early Pro Career ..........39

Chapter 6 — Hingis Dominates................................47

Chapter 7 — The Phenom Comes of Age ................58

Chapter 8 — Life in the Spotlight ............................70

Chapter 9 — The Business of Being a Star..............81

Chapter 10 — The Impact of the Phenom................88

Some of the Competition .........................................95

Glossary of Tennis Terms.........................................101

Research Sources .....................................................106

## Factsheet

**Martina Hingis**

Born in Kosice, Slovakia (then Czechoslovakia) on September 30, 1980

Residence: Trubbach, Switzerland

Height: 5' 7" (1.7 m) Weight: 130 lbs. (59 kg)

Plays: right-handed (two-handed backhand)

Languages spoken: English, German, Czech, Swiss-German

Turned Pro: October 14, 1994

Career Prizes: $6.7 million

Grand Slam Singles Titles Won: 4

1997 Grand Slam Singles Titles: Australian Open, Wimbledon, US Open

1998 Grand Slam Singles Titles: Australian Open

Singles Titles: 18

1996: Wimbledon Doubles, Porsche Grand Prix, Bank of the West

1997: Sydney International, Australian Open, Toray Pan Pacific, Open Gaz de France, Lipton, Wimbledon, Bank of the West, Toshiba, US Open, Porsche Grand Prix

1998: Sydney International Doubles, Australian Open, Toray Pan Pacific Doubles, Evert Cup, Lipton Doubles, German Grand Prix, Italian Open, French Open Doubles

## Introduction

A tennis phenomenon, a shooting star, younger and brasher than anyone else — this is the Swiss Miss, the Can't Miss Swiss, the cheerful assassin — Martina Hingis. She held the Number 1 ranking in international tennis for 80 weeks, and is still vying for first place.

She giggles with reporters. She plays with zest, with obvious enjoyment. She flashes her dazzling smile as often as her winning volleys. She shows unusual poise and maturity on the court. She throws her racket in frustration.

She speeds across the court with nimble grace, making the game look easy. Her concentration is so strong you can taste it. Her thoughts move faster than the ball, like a chess master of the tennis court. Then she loses focus and is close to tears as the match goes against her. Her feelings show. No tight-lipped, grim, grunting player, this, even in defeat.

Doggedly, she attacks another tournament, refusing to give up. She uses every shot in the tennis book unpredictably. Her mind and body perfectly in tune, she draws her opponents into their weakest position, then wins the point, the game, the set, the match, the tournament. After that, she dons tight, black, lacy gowns and parties with friends, or poses for magazine covers.

She hugs her mother, who is also her coach, saying she owes her everything. She argues with her mother, challenging every rule in her training schedule.

Is this 10 different people? No, she's only one, a remarkable one. Martina Hingis took over the Number 1 spot in the tennis world with youth, charm, and talent in 1997. She racked up win after win without alienating her public or her opponents. She grinned as she demolished other players, then often made friends of them. She has won hearts as well as titles, and that's amazing in the tennis world — a world filled with intense, ultra-serious competitors. Martina Hingis stands out from the rest.

Though ranked Number 1 in women's international professional tennis for most of 1997 and 1998, Martina was still a teenager. She was the youngest woman ever to reach Number 1 (since the rankings began), and she made it at the age of sixteen years, six months and one day. That was on March 31, 1997.

But Martina exploded into tennis history long before that. She began competing at the age of six. At the age of 12, she became the youngest-ever Grand Slam junior titlist at the 1993 tournament at Roland Garros, in France. She was the youngest junior champion ever at Wimbledon in 1994, at the age of 13.

She turned professional when she was just 14 years

old. When she captured the doubles title at Wimbledon in 1996, she was the youngest ever to win an adult title there. She was only 16 then. She was also the first Swiss woman ever to win at Wimbledon.

She became the youngest player in the 20th century to win a Grand Slam singles title at the 1997 Australian Open, aged 16. Then she won the doubles title at the same Open. This made her the first woman since Martina Navratilova's 1985 victories to win both titles.

The following year she became the youngest player to defend a Grand Slam title in the Open Era, again at the Australian Open. That gave her four Grand Slam titles, making her the youngest in this century to accomplish that feat. She won both singles and doubles titles in Australia that year.

Only Charlotte "Lottie" Dod accomplished so much so young, and Lottie Dod did it in 1888. Lottie Dod wrote the book on amazingly young athletes. She took a Wimbledon title at the age of 15 years, 10 months, a record never forgotten or beaten until Martina Hingis arrived in 1996. Dod went on to win every year she played Wimbledon. She was exceptional at other sports too, including ice skating, and field hockey. She won an Olympic medal in archery and the British Ladies Golf Championship.

Like Lottie, Martina Hingis also plays a host of other sports besides tennis. That seems to be a part of her winning combination. She has an all-round game and a varied life that other tennis players envy.

Martina really found her stride in 1996. She began to electrify the tennis world, sweeping up titles as if they were candy. And she seemed to enjoy every minute of it. She played and spoke with confidence and self-assurance when she won, and optimism when she had some defeats. Through consistent efforts, she stayed Number 1 throughout most of 1997 and 1998, in spite of some setbacks. The ranking was an achievement she wore lightly, but with pride.

There were other rewards besides the ranking. In 1996, Martina became the youngest tennis player ever, man or woman, to earn $1 million in prize money, having just turned 16. The money has been rolling in ever since. By fall 1998 she had almost $7 million in prize money, and millions more in business deals. This must have been a heady experience for one so young. Martina laughed with delight when questioned about her riches. But all this did not come as easily as it seems.

The world of professional tennis is demanding. The pressure at the top is enormous. The media attention never stops. Reporters gather after every game, asking question after question. They pester Martina at her home, on the street, in the hotels where she stays. Television crews and cameras follow her everywhere.

Then there is the pace of the tour. The tour schedule is exhausting, covering the globe. Martina has lost track of the number of jet flights she has logged, to England, Tokyo, Australia, San Diego (USA), New York, and more. Tournaments are piled up one upon the other. Tennis is a game of endurance as well as skill.

Fame produces its own pressures. Thousands praise Martina, and thousands criticize her too. Despite amazing strings of wins (37 straight in early 1997) there have been losses too. Life in the spotlight is an ego-boosting and an ego-shattering roller-coaster ride, while separated from the normal teenager's world of school, home, and friends. Few can manage the life without burning out, or exploding in anger.

Yet the word most often used of Martina is "normal." Martina commented to *Tennis* magazine in 1996, "People ask me if I miss normal life, and my answer is always the same: I feel I have a normal life, even if it's not the same life as other kids. It is maybe even better than a normal life, because my life actually is like always holidays. That's because I like tennis.

"When you win, you have a lot of happiness. When you lose, you are a little down, but tennis is not like the Olympic Games, in which you have one chance for happiness every four years. There is a new chance in tennis every week."

In spite of her jet-setting lifestyle, fame, money, and pressure don't seem to have changed Martina. How has she stayed so down-to-earth? How did she make it to the top without losing her balance? How has she survived the ups and downs without becoming a tennis brat or a tennis terror?

## Chapter 1

# Laying the Groundwork

Martina Hingis was born in Kosice, Slovakia (which was part of Czechoslovakia at that time), on September 30, 1980. Her mother, Melanie Molitor, was a tennis player who once placed tenth in the country's ratings. Molitor was still playing competitive tennis when she met Martina's father, Karol Hingis. A player himself, he coached tennis at a local club.

Martina Hingis was named after Martina Navratilova, a fellow Czechoslovakian. Navratilova was a brilliant tennis player, perhaps one of the best players of all time. She won the most titles and matches in women's tennis history. When she retired from singles competitions in 1994, she had won more than $20 million in prize money.

Navratilova was a tireless, aggressive player with a very strong net game. As her namesake, Martina Hingis had a high example to try to match. That seems to have been Molitor's intention from the beginning.

When Martina was four, her parents divorced and she moved with her mother to Roznov, Czechoslovakia.

Their new home was five hours' travel away from Kosice. Martina hardly saw her father in those years. At first this had a terrible impact on Martina. She describes it as the worst thing ever to happen to her. She missed her father and her old home. But tennis had already become a big part of her life. She settled into Roznov.

Martina was two when her mother first put a tennis racket in her hand. The little girl had just learned to walk. She used a normal-sized wooden racket that had been shaved down at the grip so she could get her tiny hand around it. They didn't practice long, only 20 minutes a day in the house. Molitor tossed the ball to her daughter, and asked her to hit it back.

Martina started playing on a real tennis court when she was three years old. She couldn't see over the net, just through the net a little. Usually she could see the ball only after it had cleared the net and was coming toward her. She was able to hit the ball back and forth to her mother 15 times. Perhaps this was the beginning of Martina's uncanny accuracy in following the ball, and her superb court sense.

Practice time increased the next year to 20 minutes on court a day. She played her first tournament at the age of four, and lost very badly. Martina laughs when she looks back at it. The tournament was for kids up to nine years old.

By the age of five, tennis was occupying more and more of Martina's time. Her mother taught tennis to kids on the clay courts of Roznov, so Martina natural-ly spent a lot of time there. And she got better. Martina won her first tournament at the age of six. She became Czechoslovakian champion in the under-9 category.

When Martina was seven, her mother married Andreas Zogg, a Swiss computer salesman. They moved to Switzerland, to a village close to her current home of Trubbach.

"That was the second-hardest time in my life," Martina told writer Dana Kennedy in 1998. "I had to go to school, but I couldn't understand anything they were saying." Martina quickly learned the Swiss-German language.

In Switzerland Martina's training was stepped up. But Molitor's coaching technique has always been unusual — strict yet flexible. Martina spent part of her day playing soccer or other games. These strengthened her and gave her agility, but they were also fun. They gave her a rounded life, with lots of competition.

Martina describes herself as lazy and calm. Her mother has been the driving force behind her tennis career. But Melanie Molitor never drove her daughter too hard. She never broke Martina's spirit. Martina was learning tennis, but she was learning to enjoy life too. She was encouraged to play with other children, not set apart.

Martina may have lost her first tournament, but her talent soon began to show. When she was nine she began to play the international tournaments for four-teen-year-olds. At 10 she started to win some of these tournaments.

A turning point came when she was 11 and began to win over her mother. This was horribly embarrassing at first, and Martina didn't want to play against her mom anymore. Molitor had a different reaction. She brought in a talented young man to play Martina, to challenge her even more.

When Martina was 11 she won the European Championships. She was consistently beating older players. The early training, the years of preparation, were bearing fruit.

Her amateur career took off in 1993. She began to attract attention. She was only 12 when she won the Junior French Open — a phenomenal victory in an event open to 18-year-olds. Martina was the youngest person ever to win it, beating the previous record-holder, Jennifer Capriati.

At 13 Martina won the Junior US Open and the Wimbledon Junior Tournament. She was the youngest to win that Wimbledon junior title. In 1994 Martina was named International Tennis Federation Junior Girls Singles Champion.

Her future seemed clear. Martina Hingis turned professional on October 14, 1994, at the age of 14.

## Chapter 2

# The Power Behind the Star

"She was born to play tennis. You cannot work at this. Even if you work at it, you cannot have it like she has it," said Irina Spirlea, who lost to Martina during the 1997 Australian Open.

Born for it? Maybe. Both her parents played tennis. Martina may have inherited a body well suited to the game and a talent for sports. But there's more to it than that.

They say there's a power behind every great person. Melanie Molitor is the power behind Martina — her mother, coach, and best friend, the one who has pushed from the beginning. Why?

Molitor herself began playing tennis at the age of seven. She watched Martina Navratilova when they were teens playing in local tournaments. They didn't play each other, and they didn't know each other. But Molitor watched with envy as Navratilova left Czechoslovakia, and won titles, honors, fame, and riches. Melanie Molitor began to see tennis as a way out of Czechoslovakia.

Melanie had good reason to want to leave. When she was growing up, Czechoslovakia had a communist government. There were many restrictions on the lives of its citizens. Molitor's father was a landscape architect. He opposed the communist government. He wanted a different form of government, more like those of western countries. He and his friends talked of the western way of life, outside of Czechoslovakia.

In the late 1940s, Mr. Molitor's anti-government activities came to the notice of the authorities. He had given shelter to a friend running from the police. Mr. Molitor was arrested, tried, and sentenced. He endured eight years of hard labor in a uranium mine.

Melanie Molitor says these years were shattering for her father. He was never the same afterward. The impact on Molitor and her family was devastating. She idolized her father, who had risked so much for his anti-government point of view, and suffered so much. She longed for a western lifestyle.

But if you didn't like life in Czechoslovakia, it was difficult to leave. The government put limits on who was allowed to travel outside the nation's borders. And even if you could travel, it was often too expensive for an average citizen to do so.

One way to get around these limits was to become an athlete — a very good athlete. Then the government would sponsor you. You could travel to other countries to compete in events like the Olympics.

Sometimes athletes would use these occasions as a chance to escape — to defect. Once they were outside the country, they would refuse to return. They would decide to live in another country, such as the USA, where athletes could make their own decisions about their careers and training. Martina Navratilova is one example of an athlete who made the decision to defect.

Melanie Molitor would have liked to follow Navratilova's example, but she wasn't good enough to defect. She had to abandon her dream of using tennis as a way out of Czechoslovakia.

Instead, from the time Molitor became pregnant, she planned for her child to become a tennis star. Like many parents, she wanted her child to have the things she had once dreamed of having — the choices and riches Molitor had not enjoyed.

Molitor has devoted her life to making Martina a tennis superstar. She told her daughter that she would become the best so often that Martina came to believe it too. Martina adopted her mother's goal, without being forced.

Far from being laid back, Molitor has a fiery temperament. But she doesn't seem to show her temper with her daughter. She speaks quietly to her at training or warm-up sessions. Molitor has the drive and ambition, and she certainly makes the rules. But she holds back from pushing her daughter too far, too fast. When experts said working on a power serve might damage

Martina's still-developing back and shoulders, Molitor held her back.

While other tennis parents force their children to endure hours of grinding drill, Molitor encourages Martina to enjoy other sports. Molitor sees the big picture, not just a tennis trophy. This is a rare combination in tennis parent-coaches.

Molitor seems harsh to some people. She doesn't try to spare other people's feelings (a characteristic Martina seems to have as well). But she learns everything she can from other coaches, and isn't afraid to change her mind. And her own love of tennis has never deserted her.

Mother and daughter travel everywhere together. They chat warmly in Czech to one another, often hugging. The affection between them is obvious. Deep love is the cornerstone of their relationship. They are a team.

Molitor has not forgotten that she is a mother first, and a coach second. "Above all we must save the friendship," Molitor says. "We like what we're doing."

The warmth between them showed when Molitor leaped out of the stands to hug Martina after the 1997 Australian singles victory.

There have been clashes, too, especially as Martina got older. During Martina's first year on the pro tour, she rebelled and wouldn't follow the training schedule. She thought success would come anyway. Then she began to lose matches, notably the first round of the Lipton Championships.

Molitor got tough. She gave her daughter a choice: Martina could go back to school or work harder on tennis. But Molitor also told her that tennis wasn't the most important thing — it never was. Tennis was the chance for Martina to have a good life. If Martina decided against tennis, Molitor said she would love her anyway. It was up to Martina to decide for herself. What did she want?

Already Martina had begun to enjoy the life tennis brought them. Martina decided to keep on playing tennis. She went on to dominate 1997 women's tennis as no one so young had done before.

Now they debate everything as Martina grows older. "We have a great relationship," Martina told an interviewer from *Vogue* magazine."We're very close. We have little fights, sure. But no problem. We end up laughing." Martina is the first to say that she owes everything to her mother.

## Chapter 3

# Tennis Close-Up:
# A Pro's Technique

The experts call her a "phenom," a tennis teen queen. No one denies her talent.

Martina isn't particularly big or powerful. She's usually playing with women taller than she. These women have a longer reach, or blindingly fast serves. Venus Williams, at six feet, one-and-a-half inches (1.88 metres), with a 120-mph (190-km/hr) serve, has more size and power. Yet Martina has beaten her. How?

Tennis is an easy game, in theory. Take a ball, about two and a half inches (64 millimetres) in diameter, made of rubber and covered with a fabric blend of Dacron, nylon, and wool. It should weigh just over two ounces (57 grams). Hit the ball over a net strung across the rectangular court. Make sure it lands on or within the lines marking the edges of the playing field, but also make sure the other player can't hit it back. Simple, right? Wrong!

A very early version of tennis was played with the hands, a sort of handball game. As early cavemen

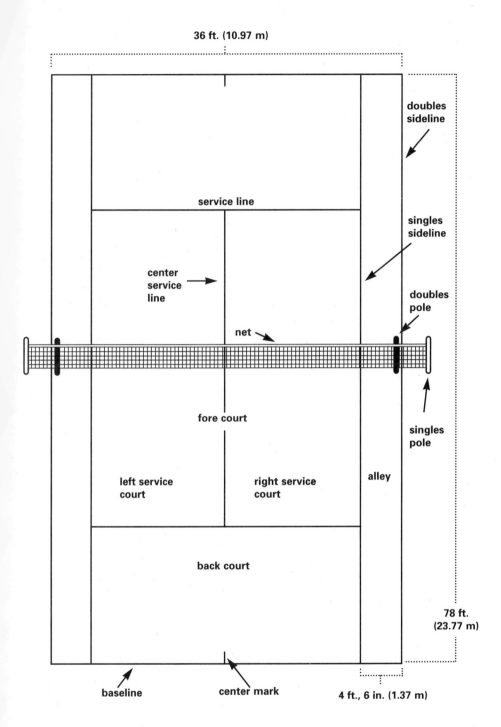

36 ft. (10.97 m)

doubles sideline

singles sideline

service line

center service line

doubles pole

net

singles pole

fore court

left service court

right service court

alley

back court

baseline

center mark

4 ft., 6 in. (1.37 m)

78 ft. (23.77 m)

found, tools add power to an action. With the racket, tennis players have a longer reach, and can put more clout into the ball. They can make the ball spin so it will drop more quickly or travel farther.

But the court is still a big space to cover in the time it takes the ball to fly through the air. Players have to move quickly, with speed and agility. Covering that much territory so quickly can tire you out, so physical endurance is important, too.

Many factors come into play in winning on the court, but perhaps the two most important are *power* and *tactics.* Power means making the ball travel fast. The faster the ball travels, the better. Make it travel so fast that it whizzes past your opponent. She may be unable to react quickly enough to return it.

To achieve power, players have to be strong and fit. They must also use the dynamics of their bodies and the rackets well. The speed of the ball isn't determined just by hitting the ball hard. It's also determined by *how* you hit the ball.

Tactics in tennis involve catching your opponent off guard, making it difficult for them to hit the ball. This requires both physical and mental skills. First, you must be able to send the ball to a particular spot. This is called "placement" and it can give you control of the points.

Every player prefers to play from certain parts of the court. If you can identify the shots your opponent handles poorly, the places on the court she cannot reach in time, the places where she does not seem comfortable, then that is where you try to send the ball. This requires accuracy. The more accurate you are in placing the ball, the more control you have over the game.

The advantages of placement aren't as obvious as they seem. For instance, some players are "baseline players." The baseline is the line that runs along the back of the court. Baseline players like to stay near the back of the court and use "ground shots," hitting the ball after it has bounced. They aren't very good at "volleying," which means hitting the ball back before it bounces. If you can make the ball bounce very near a baseline player's side of the net, then she is forced to approach the net to return it. You've made her go outside her comfort zone. Force her to volley next and you may make her use a shot she doesn't handle well. Her shot might go wide, heading out of the court. Another point won. By making her use her weakest shots, your control of the game increases.

The unexpected is a big tactic in the game, too, and not simply achieved. Each player looks at how the ball is travelling, and tries to guess where her opponent will place the ball on the return shot. Here the player is tracking the ball — its speed, its angle, its spin, the angle of the return stroke. The player makes a very rapid prediction, then runs to where she thinks the ball is coming, ready to return it.

The crowning achievement of a player with good "court sense" is to be there, ready to return the ball accurately, powerfully, and in a way that puts her opponent on the defensive. Do this well enough, and it's as if you have a crystal ball in your head, as if you can see into the future. If you can anticipate, and use an unexpected return shot, you have taken over control of the game. In short, surprise your opponent, but don't let her surprise you.

Put all of this together, and you have tactics. These two components of the game — the speed of the ball, or "power" as it is usually called, and tactics are still the tennis players' stock in trade. Power is in the speed of serves and returns; tactics in the choice of shot, placement, and where the player chooses to receive the shot, anticipating her opponent's move. Those choices make or break a champion. And they have to be made with a speed that puts computers to shame. How a player uses these tools of the game defines her.

What is Martina's technique? Tactics head the list. Martina uses her head. She thinks on the court. Martina's game shows anticipation and planning. When she selects what shot to use and where to receive her opponent's shot, she shows a champion's judgment. You can almost see her calculating how to return the ball or which serve to use.

She also looks for the weakest part of her opponent's game. Players like American star Lindsay

Davenport tend to stay back from the net. Martina has forced Davenport out of her comfort zone by landing balls close to the net.

What if a player charges the net with confidence? To counter this move Martina will land the ball far back, or on the side of the court her opponent least expects. By playing "down the line" — returning the ball on the same side of the court, instead of diagonally across the court, Martina has often surprised her opponents. She can land the ball so far away from where it was expected that it cannot be returned. In this way, a defensive shot can sometimes be turned into an offensive shot.

A game based on tactics makes tennis a bit like chess. If it is chess, Martina has shown herself to be a chess master many times — seeming older and wiser than her years.

Martina doesn't like to drag out the game, either. She goes for points quickly. Having more than one idea puts her ahead of a lot of the younger players, who may not have learned how to plan ahead yet. Martina doesn't go into her games blind. Usually she has watched her opponents play before, or has faced them on the court. She already knows the kind of game she will face, and selects a variety of tactics that may give her control of the game.

Martina is light on her feet. By playing the game with her head, she is able to be economical in the way she uses her body. This imparts a graceful, effortless appearance to her game, a far cry from the grunting, sledge-hammer efforts of players like Steffi Graf. Martina's moves are agile. She keeps her body erect. This allows her to keep her attention riveted on the ball. Razor-sharp concentration is the key. She is able to track the ball from the instant it is struck by her opponent's racket, decide where it's going, and react without hesitation. When she's at her best, Martina's concentration allows her to out-manoeuvre the opposition.

Martina seems comfortable in every part of the court. Most of today's players prefer to play from certain positions. Martina can switch from ground strokes delivered from the rear of the court, to net-nudging volleys. By varying her shots so widely, she can wear down her opponents, forcing them to run all over the court. She's a quick-change artist, in tennis terms, able to pull any shot out of her bag of tricks. She is an all-round player.

When she needs to, Martina can move fast. She'll dash from the backcourt to the net in seconds, or vice versa. Speed on her feet is another key to her success. There's a lot of risk in playing so close to the net. There's less time to go after the ball, and less margin for error in anticipating where the ball will approach. Few of her opponents are willing to take the risk. Martina dares.

"The closer I am to the net, the easier it is to hit a winner," Martina told *Sport* magazine. "At net, I'm always ready to react to anything — passing shots, lobs and even when my opponent tries to hit the ball right at me. Preparation is the key. I can't hesitate when I go to the net. I begin moving when I see my opponent hitting a defensive shot."

Her daring shows in other ways too. Even on the slippery grass of Wimbledon in practice warm-ups, she has run full tilt, pumping her arms like a sprinter. Nothing was held back. Others might fear injury and slow down.

This combination of versatility, court cunning, and boldness allows Martina to surprise her competitors. And it's not just that she can make the shots. The way she makes them counts too. Molitor has taught her top techniques.

If a karate master tries to break a brick using only the strength of his forearm, the brick is more likely to break *him*. What makes the brick break is that the power of the master's whole body is applied to the blow. Physical strength is not nearly as important as how he puts his whole body strength into the blow — his body mechanics.

Similarly, in tennis, Martina has been able to dominate because of the way she uses her whole body to drive the balls. She uses superb body mechanics. She twists her body in readiness to strike the ball, rotating hips or shoulders. She is like a spring, coiled to strike as the ball hurtles toward her. Then she unleashes all of that force through her arm and into the motion of the racket. You can see her readiness in her bent knees, in her open stance as she faces the net dead on, in the positioning of the racket behind her, in the distribution of her weight. She may be lighter than her opponents, but she makes every bit count.

Surprisingly, one of the secrets of great tennis is not in having strong arms, but in having strong legs. The biggest, strongest muscles of the body are in the legs and buttocks. Harnessing this strength is one of the secrets of great body mechanics. Martina has very strong legs. She does a lot of leg exercises to strengthen her hamstring muscles, so she can stay low and use good body mechanics.

There are other advantages too. She is able to keep her balance because she moves with her legs, like a dancer, her weight balanced over her feet. This allows her to respond quickly to the next shot. She's balanced even on the run, keeping the racket in front of her. Other players may bend from the waist or lunge. Then they have to take steps to recover their balance.

Martina uses a western or semi-western grip on her racket. She doesn't strangle the racket by gripping too tightly. She has "soft hands." Too tight a grip gives rigidity to the wrist action. Martina has avoided this pitfall. As she strikes the ball she can snap her wrist into her forehand, adding power to the shot. She can also apply spin to the ball, causing it to fall sooner, as in a drop shot, or travel farther.

Like all the great players, Martina wants to be the best, she wants to win. During a two-hour rain delay in the 1996 US Open, she played games of cards, backgammon, and Parcheesi in the players' lounge. Some players might have paced. She didn't. She's competitive, and yet relaxed.

According to Martina Navratilova, "her greatest shot is her down-the-line off the crosscourt. It's unmatched." This is a shot that travels to the same side of the court after crossing the net, instead of across the court.

Summing up, Martina does not play like Martina Navratilova, after whom she was named. She plays more like Chris Evert, Navratilova's strongest competitor. Navratilova played aggressively, serving powerfully and volleying. Evert had a stellar career, tied with Navratilova for major titles. But Evert usually played a tactics game from the baseline, staying back from the net and looking for the opportunity to score. Martina is no baseliner, but as a tactician, with speed, technique, and endurance, she is like Evert.

Evert says, "Martina has a lot of the qualities I had. But she is a better and more complete player than I was because she knows how to volley."

Weaknesses? Martina learned the game on red clay courts. Tennis courts may be made of differing surfaces

— among them hard (perhaps asphalt or concrete), clay, carpet, or grass. The way the players move and the way the ball bounces in play varies according to the court surfaces. Some players tend to play better on one surface. Martina has had to adjust to the speed of the hard courts. She can't slide to the ball as she did on clay. But she seems to have made adjustments. She's won on all court surfaces, now — hard, clay, grass, carpet.

Power players can put her in a defensive position, by hitting the ball very hard from the first. Martina admits she doesn't like this, and has lost some matches this way.

Martina Navratilova analyzed Hingis's style for *Tennis* magazine in 1997. Navratilova thinks her emotions might be a bigger problem. "Martina plays great when she's ahead, but as soon as things don't go her way, she falls apart. I can relate because I used to be that way. Then [tennis star] Billie Jean King taught me to play one game at a time. Martina can fix it, too."

## Chapter 4

# Going Pro:
# A Controversial Move

The earliest tennis matches were played in 1873 in England. Major Walter Clopton Wingfield patented tennis equipment and rules in 1874. The game was played on a grass court. Soon it was called lawn tennis, and became popular very quickly. In 1877 the All England Croquet Club changed its name to the All England Croquet and Lawn Tennis Club. That same year the club sponsored the first major tennis tournament at the club's headquarters. That was in Wimbledon, a suburb of London.

It was the beginning of the world's most respected tennis tournament. Many think of the Wimbledon tournament as the unofficial world championship in tennis — the "Big W." This applies to men, women, and children, to singles and doubles. Up to 40,000 people a day gather to watch the 13-day Wimbledon Tournament each year. Millions more follow it on television. So many reporters cover the event that limits have to be set. Its earliest home is still tennis's most glamorous site. Winners there are said to have won crowns, like royalty.

After its invention, tennis spread quickly to France, to the United States, and around the world. International tennis got a boost with the donation of the Davis Cup by American player Dwight Davis. It goes to the country that wins the most world men's championships. Women's tennis didn't have as much prestige at first.

Most tennis is played by amateurs. They do it for fun and receive no money. In professional tennis, cash prizes, as well as trophies, are awarded for the big tournaments.

It was only in the 1960s that professional tennis became accepted. Until 1968 only amateurs could play in major tournaments. That year, the International Tennis Federation (ITF) voted to allow amateurs and professionals to play in the same tournaments. These tournaments were called "open" tournaments. Now almost all major tournaments are open. The years from 1968 on are called the "Open Era" of tennis.

In 1972 women professional tennis players formed the Women's Tennis Association (WTA). The WTA supervises the women's professional tour.

The prize money awarded to women who win tournaments used to be much less than that awarded to men. Billie Jean King was part of a fight to make the awards equal. Billie Jean was a top player in the 1960s and '70s. She was an all-time Wimbledon champion with 20 wins. In 1973 she defeated a top-ranked male player, Bobby Riggs, in a televised tennis game, a "battle of the sexes."

That game helped show that the quality of women's tennis was equal to that of men's tennis, and that therefore women players should receive the same kind of prize money that the men did. The prize money for women was raised by most tournaments after that, though usually not to the same levels as that received by the male players.

Today, both women and men compete for enormous sums. When she won the 1997 US Open singles title, Martina Hingis took home $650,000, while the runner-up got $350,000 — the same amounts won by the respective male players in the same competition.

Tennis players have become stars on the world stage. As the world watches tennis tournaments on television, leading players become millionaires. Fame and prestige go to the winners. And the winners keep getting younger. Enormous publicity as well as money are involved. Tennis has become a game of nerves as well as skill, with a lot of pressure to succeed. Tennis stars are loved and hated by the public.

This is the world Martina Hingis entered at the age of 14, when she became a professional. There was a lot of controversy over Martina going pro at such an early age. Young players before her had been unable to handle the pressure of professional tennis. Andrea Jaeger and Tracy Austin were very gifted players in the '70s and '80s who also turned pro at a young age. They got a lot of attention for their abilities, and did very well at first. But after their first flashes of brilliance, they began to have trouble. They "burned out" in a short time, and almost disappeared from the tour.

The most serious example of a player taking on too much at an early age was Jennifer Capriati. Capriati became a pro at the age of 13 years, 11 months. In her first year she beat five players in the Top Ten and entered the Top Ten list herself. But as her career progressed she began to have troubles off the court. She began shoplifting and taking drugs. Eventually she had to take time off from her career to go to a drug rehabilitation center.

Many people concluded from these cases that it was a mistake to push children into professional athletics too soon. If players begin the grueling professional tour too young, they may lose their love of the sport. Teenagers were good enough to beat adult players, but the stresses seemed to be too much.

Martina Hingis was still wearing braces on her teeth when she became a pro. She was just starting the eighth grade. She was a child entering a tough adult world. But she was relaxed, at home with the older players, the cameras, and microphones. She seemed mature for her age, and unworried. What about the girls who had burned out at a young age? What about Capriati's problems with drugs? "She's just one person," Martina responded. "There are a thousand girls in the [professional] rankings."

Martina didn't seem concerned about entering the world of professional tennis, and neither did her mother. For Martina to go pro seemed a natural development. They had been working for this for 10 years already.

Martina had signed a five-year contract with an agency 18 months before she turned pro. The agency had already arranged for Martina to represent a number of companies in exchange for large sums of money. Her agents wanted Martina to become professional because it would make her even more attractive to advertisers.

But the WTA was concerned about young players turning pro too soon. The association decided to introduce new age restrictions beginning in 1995. Fourteen-year-olds would be able to play only five professional events per year. Players aged 15 to 17 would be introduced gradually to big events. Fifteen-year-olds could play eight. Only at age 18 would all limits be removed.

For Martina and others who beat the deadline for these new rules, the WTA had other plans. The association offered career and psychological counseling to the young players. Also they would be monitored for their physical health. So Martina has a WTA mentor — Chris Evert. But her chief protector will be, as always, her mother.

How does Molitor plan to protect Martina from stress and burn-out? By being flexible and keeping things simple. By keeping other sports and activities a part of Martina's life. Will it work? Only time can answer that question.

Venus Williams, a tall, powerful USA tennis player, became pro at the same time as Martina. Williams, too, avoided the new WTA rules. Other young talents, like the Russian, Anna Kournikova, have to follow the new rules and play fewer tournaments, which means fewer chances to gain professional experience and win big prize money. These players feel they are being treated unfairly.

Upset by the new rules, a group of players tried to take over the WTA board. Some of the top players including Martina, Monica Seles, and Steffi Graf took legal action to stop this take-over. Debate about the age issue continues. The controversy shows that there is more to professional tennis than just hitting a ball around. Politics is part of the adult tennis world Martina joined. It's a big, complicated world. How will Martina fare in it?

## Chapter 5

# A Star Rising: Early Pro Career

In her early pro career, the action heated up for Martina Hingis. The world began to really take notice of the talented teen.

In 1995 she won her first WTA doubles title at the Hamburg Open with Gigi Fernandez. Then Martina's name hit the headlines. She won a singles match at the Australian Open. She was the youngest female player in the Open Era to do this, at 14 years, four months. Her highest ranking in 1995 was 16th. She had jumped from 86th place in a year. This was extraordinary. The Corel WTA Tour gave her the Most Impressive Newcomer award. *Tennis* magazine named her 1995 Female Rookie of the Year.

In 1996 Martina advanced steadily. Her amateur career had given her a solid foundation. Her experience began to show. She was poised and steady in play, even against the best players. She competed as part of the Swiss Olympic team. She won no medals, but she gained valuable experience. Martina worked hard, but had fun too.

There are four major tennis championships each year: the Australian Open, the French Open, Wimbledon, and the US Open. Winning all four events is called a "Grand Slam," so they are each known as Grand Slam tournaments. Martina reached her first-ever Grand Slam quarterfinal at the Australian Open in 1996. She was only 15 years old. Older and more experienced players were losing to her. Martina was obviously enjoying herself on the court. She was on her way.

She reached the semifinals in the Pan Pacific singles, finally losing to her friend Iva Majoli. Her disappointing loss in the first round of the Lipton Championships in March proved to be a turning point. Martina began to train harder and reached the final in the Italian Open in May.

Most people saw these as big accomplishments. For Martina, they were just warm-ups. She hit Wimbledon with an explosion of energy and confidence. She knew she was ready for the Big W.

She reached the quarterfinals in the singles and won the Wimbledon doubles title with Helena Sukova. This made her the youngest player ever to win an adult Wimbledon title, at age 15 years, 282 days, beating Charlotte Dod's record. Martina also became the first Swiss woman to win a Wimbledon crown.

In a strong bid for the US Open, Martina advanced to the semifinals, where she was defeated by Steffi Graf.

Martina's first WTA singles title wasn't long in coming. She won the Porsche Tennis Grand Prix, in Filderstadt, Germany. There she defeated three top players — Number 2 Arantxa Sanchez Vicario, Number 5 Anke Huber, and Number 6 Lindsay Davenport. She was too young to drive the Porsche she won.

At the European Indoor Championship in Zurich, she again won the doubles title with Helena Sukova, though she lost the singles title to Jana Novotna in the final round. She was now consistently battling to the top ranks.

In one of the biggest upsets of the year, Martina won the singles title at the Bank of the West Classic, in Oakland, California, over Monica Seles, in straight sets, 6-2, 6-0, in less than an hour. Seles was coming back to tennis after a terrible injury. But Seles was still one of the strongest of the experienced, older players.

Seles spotted Martina's strength. "I think she is very tough mentally, which is unusual for a girl her age." During the Classic, Martina became the youngest tennis player ever, man or woman, to earn $1 million in prize money.

The season-ending Chase Championships features just 16 of the top women players of the year. At the 1996 Championships, Martina battled Steffi Graf, who was ranked Number 1 at the time. She had bested Graf in the quarterfinals of the Italian Open, but lost to Graf at the US Open. Who would prevail in the Chase tournament? Martina fought Graf for a grueling five sets before losing — an incredible show.

The Corel WTA Tour named Martina 1996 Most Improved Player. She made it into the world's Top 10 singles rankings on October 7, 1996, just one week after her 16th birthday. She became the fifth-youngest player in the Open Era to crack the Top 10 in world rankings, after Jennifer Capriati, Tracy Austin, Andrea Jaeger, and Monica Seles. Martina's highest ranking in 1996 was fourth.

Martina gets a hug from her mother and coach, Melanie Molitor, after winning the final of the Australian Open Tennis Championships in January 1997. It was Martina's first Grand Slam win.

Martina watches her shot on the way to defeating Monica Seles for the Family Circle Magazine Cup tennis tournament championship in South Carolina in April 1997.

Martina Hingis smiles with her defeated opponent, Jana Novotna of the Czech Republic, after their Women's Singles final at Wimbledon in 1997. Martina won the final 2–6, 6–3, 6–3 to become the youngest winner ever.

Martina hugs the Australian Open trophy after winning the final against Conchita Martinez of Spain, in Melbourne in January 1998.

# Chapter 6

# Hingis Dominates

The year 1997 belonged to Martina Hingis. She ruled women's tennis, sweeping up titles and honors with ease. Her performance was staggering. Incredibly, she won 37 straight matches to start the season, the second-best start in the Open Era. By the end of the tennis season she had won 75 matches in total, more than anyone else on the tour for the year.

She was named 1997 Player of the Year by the Corel WTA Tour, the International Tennis Federation and *Tennis* magazine, and the Associated Press named her Female Athlete of the Year. She was Chase Monthly Champion for January, March, and July, having the most wins each month.

So outstanding was her performance that Martina's mother was named 1997 Coach of the Year by the Swiss Sports Federation, becoming the first woman to win the award. *Tennis* honored Molitor too, giving her the title of 1997 Coach of the Year.

The season opened in January in Australia. First Martina took down the former teen prodigy Jennifer

Capriati of the USA in the Sydney International. Playing on a hard court outdoors, Capriati seemed to recover in the second set, winning it 5–7 over Martina. But Martina trounced her in the decisive third set, 6–1.

At the Australian Open in Melbourne, Martina cruised through the qualifying matches to the finals in spite of a fall from horseback off the courts. She and Natasha Zvereva teamed up for the doubles. They defeated third-seeded Lindsay Davenport and Lisa Raymond in straight sets. All through the match, Martina smiled playfully.

The next day she had a bigger reason to smile as she smashed the record books. It took her only 59 minutes to take the singles title over France's Mary Pierce. Pierce's powerful ground strokes were no match for Martina's precision and delicate drop shots — she could make the ball drop just over the net, forcing Pierce to dash forward to meet the ball.

With these victories Martina became the youngest player in the twentieth century to win a Grand Slam title. She was also the first woman to win both Australian Open titles since Martina Navratilova, and the youngest woman ever to take the Australian Open doubles title. Martina was only 16 years old. No Swiss woman had ever won a Grand Slam singles title before.

The end of January saw Martina in Tokyo, at the Toray Pan Pacific Open. She won the women's early round matches and seemed unstoppable. In the finals she was to face 27-year-old Steffi Graf of Germany, still ranked Number 1 in the world.

But Graf had been struggling with injuries, and in her semifinal match she aggravated a knee injury. She withdrew from the finals. Martina took the Pan Pacific title by default. Speculation continues over this win. How would 1997 have looked for Martina if Graf had been fit to compete? No one can answer this question.

The tournament schedule allows no time for injuries to heal, or for winners to gloat. The day after the Pan Pacific ended, the Open Gaz de France began in Paris. There Martina captured the singles and doubles titles, repeating her Australian triumph.

The news was full of adulation for the new tennis sensation. Martina had become the first woman to win consecutive tournaments on three continents — Australia (Sydney and Australian Open), Asia (Pan Pacific Open), and Europe (Open Gaz de France). The last player to accomplish this feat was Boris Becker in 1986.

The eyes of the tennis world were on Martina as she flew to Florida, USA, in mid-March to play in the Lipton Championships. Her performance was light years beyond the previous year's Lipton, where she had lost in the first rounds. After an easy victory over Venus Williams in the third round, she joked with reporters, tossing them a hair bead Williams had dropped during the match. "I have a present for you. One of Venus's pearls." But she recognized Williams's potential. "For sure she is going to be a good player."

In the finals Martina defeated the veteran power player Monica Seles in straight sets, 6-2, 6-1 in only 44 minutes. It was an impressive victory. Martina also made the $1 million mark in prize money for 1997, with the Lipton purse. This was the fastest accumulation of prize money in a year by any woman player ever.

Later in March came the Family Circle Cup at Hilton Head, South Carolina, USA. Again Martina breezed through the early round matches to face Monica Seles. Their match was longer this time, and hard fought. Seles won five games to open the match. Martina lost the first set.

Martina was visibly upset by this reversal. She regained control, taking the lead in the second set. She also committed errors, temporarily falling behind. She was tiring. But with varied, accurate shots she came back to win the second, and then the third set, taking the title. Playing with Mary Joe Fernandez, Martina defeated Lindsay Davenport and Jana Novotna in the doubles.

Her winnings at the Family Circle Cup shot Martina to the top of the ratings. On March 31, 1997, Martina became the youngest female tennis player to be ranked Number 1 since the Tour's computer rankings began in 1975, at age 16 years and 6 months.

It seemed in March of 1997 that nothing could stop Martina. She was sweeping the tennis titles and record books like a small tornado. Then she received her first serious injury.

On April 21, 1997, Martina fell off a horse in Switzerland, only four months following her previous fall. Martina had been lucky then. No harm had been done by her first spill in January 1997, and she had won the Australian Open after that. Martina must have felt invincible.

But this second fall was more serious. It caused a slight tear in one of the ligaments in her left knee that would need surgery to fix. The operation was performed on April 23. Martina was off the tour for seven weeks and had to withdraw from tournaments in Hamburg, Berlin, and Rome.

Horseback riding is one of Martina's passions. She once even dreamed of being a show-jumping champion. In the mountains of her Swiss home, she rides her horses full out, with no holding back. With the knee injury, she was paying for her fearless behavior.

Was it foolhardy to take risks riding horses in the middle of the most important year in her tennis career? Some say so. But part of Martina's recipe for success is risk-taking. By living a life wider than the tennis court, Martina expands her athletic experience and her enthusiasm. She brings all of this back to the tennis court. Without it, she would be a very different player.

Martina worked hard to regain her old form after the surgery. By May she was practicing on court again. She went into the French Open, at Roland Garros, at the end of the month. This was one of the Majors, a Grand Slam tournament played on clay. The pressure was on to see how Martina would perform.

At first she seemed to be her old self. She took on Arantxa Sanchez Vicario in the quarterfinals, and Seles in the semifinals. She defeated them both. Then in the finals Iva Majoli of Croatia crushed her.

Nineteen-year-old Majoli sent brutal ground strokes and powerful serves against Martina. Martina took a bathroom break and later a timeout to deal with cramps in her leg. Her shots went wild. She couldn't gain the offensive. When one of her forehands hit the net she was so frustrated she tossed her racket. The spectators booed her. The match didn't go to a third set. It was the most humiliating defeat Martina had suffered all year.

As always, reporters wanted her comments. They expected her to show a host of negative feelings. Instead Martina recovered enough composure to congratulate Majoli, thank her mother, and speak positively about reaching the final after her injury. She showed she could be cool in defeat, something a champion needs.

Staying at the top means being able to take setbacks in stride, go on and try to do better. Martina seemed determined to do that. A lot of major tournaments lay ahead, loaded with opportunities for triumphs and humiliations. A great tennis player learns to regain her confidence and overcome setbacks.

This setback was a serious one, though. Without the French Open title, Martina could not take all the 1997 Majors. The accident may have cost Martina a Grand Slam sweep. She lost in the doubles as well at the French Open.

Late June saw Martina at the Wimbledon Championships, London, playing on grass. Clay was Martina's favorite surface, grass the surface on which she had the least experience. Everyone wondered how she would fare. Her mental discipline, her emotions, and her skills would be stretched to their limits.

Facing Jana Novotna of the Czech Republic, a superb grass-court player, perhaps the best serve and volley player today, Martina lost the first set. During the second set Martina started to show her range of play. She was outstanding in the backcourt, but she rushed the net, too. She ripped backhand passes, used her forehand lob, and returned strong forehand volleys to break Novotna's game.

She won the singles 2–6, 6–3, 6–3. This made her the youngest player in the Open Era to win a Wimbledon singles title, at 16 years, nine months. She was also the first Swiss woman ever to win the Wimbledon singles.

Martina was back on top. She had the crown most respected throughout the tennis world.

At the Bank of the West Classic in Stanford, USA, in late July, Martina kept her opponent Conchita Martinez on the defensive. Most of her first serves were successful, and she didn't commit any double faults. The tired Martinez had been up until past midnight the night before playing a late doubles match. Martina played aggressively, winning the match in straight sets, 6–0, 6–2. The elated Martina grabbed the tournament mascot, a big, brown stuffed toy bear, before taking the winner's trophy — for a moment, all kid.

Then she teamed up with Lindsay Davenport to win the doubles over Conchita Martinez and Patricia Tarabini. Spectators were beginning to wonder if Martina Hingis could do anything wrong.

At the end of July Martina took her ninth title of the year at the Toshiba Classic in San Diego, USA. Martina had more of a fight, but she still triumphed over Seles, 7–6, 6–4. "She's just playing some great tennis," the former No. 1 Seles said of Martina. Hingis also won the doubles with Arantxa Sanchez Vicario.

Then in August, at the Acura Classic in Los Angeles, USA, Martina was defeated by Lindsay Davenport in the semifinals, 2–6, 6–4, 4–6. The six-foot (1.83-m) Davenport, with her powerful serves, turned the tables on Martina. It must have been a shock for the teen sensation. Commentators wondered how Martina would react.

She showed them in the US Open at Flushing Meadows, New York. Only two weeks after the Acura, Martina made the final and faced Venus Williams, a tall, powerful player, though unseeded. They were the youngest finalists in Grand Slam history — Williams was 17.

Martina kept the ball in play through long rallies, and looked for her chance to make point. She showed confidence and aggression, varying the shots. Her games were almost flawless. She defeated Williams 6–0, 6–4, to take the title. It was an electrifying victory, placing Martina in the record books. She held the victor's cup high. "The big names are on it. One of them is mine," she said, grinning triumphantly.

By winning, she became second-youngest US Championship winner at 16 years, 11 months. (Tracy Austin was 16 years, nine months old when she won the title in 1979.) Only five other players have won three or more Grand Slam singles titles in a calendar year in the Open Era (Court, Graf, King, Navratilova, and Seles). Martina joined Steffi Graf and Monica Seles as the only teenagers in the Open Era to win three or more Grand Slam titles in one year. Martina also became the first woman to earn over $3 million in prize money in one season.

She lost the US Open doubles in semifinals with Sanchez Vicario to Davenport and Novotna. But in the glory of her wins, that hardly mattered.

In Germany at the Sparkassen Cup, Martina lost the singles in the semifinals to Amanda Croetzer. But she won the doubles with Jana Novotna over Yayuk Basuki and Helena Sukova.

Another week, another chance — that's the nature of tennis. The Porsche Grand Prix in Filderstadt, Germany, had been good to Martina in 1996. There she had won her first WTA singles title. In early October of 1997, she swept the singles and the doubles in Filderstadt, defending her title and winning another Porsche, well ahead of the Swiss legal driving age of 18. She defeated Lisa Raymond of the USA for the singles title in straight sets, 6–4, 6–2. Never one to hide her feelings, Martina was jubilant.

Then she won the doubles with Arantxa Sanchez Vicario over Lindsay Davenport and Jana Novotna after a long-fought game. This was the sixth time in the year Martina won both the singles and the doubles titles in the same tournament — a remarkable achievement.

A day later, Martina was in Zurich, Switzerland, for the European Indoor Championships. The pace of the tournament schedule might have begun to affect even the energetic teen. She was defeated in the quarterfinals by Lisa Raymond, whom she had beaten only weeks ago in Germany. Martina showed endurance, though. She teamed up with Arantxa Sanchez Vicario to reach and then win the doubles title.

At the Advanta Championships in Philadelphia, USA, in November, Martina seemed to struggle. She needed three sets in quarterfinals and semifinals to win. In the finals she played three sets, including two tie breaks against Lindsay Davenport, but came out victorious. Why the struggle? Martina had taken three weeks off before the Advanta. She had suffered a slight foot injury, and admitted she had felt overconfident.

The competition seemed to humble Martina a little. She saw she wasn't the only player who could deliver on the courts. As if to underline that point, she lost in the doubles.

A slightly deflated Martina lost in November at the season-closing Chase Championships in New York, first in singles to Mary Pierce of France, in the quarterfinals, 6–3, 2–6, 7–5, then in the doubles.

But nothing could take away the triumphs of 1997, the new records she had set, and the ranking she had won. Martina came out of 1997 Number 1, forever written in the tennis history books as a brilliant young player, a phenomenon, a tennis sensation.

## Chapter 7

# The Phenom Comes of Age

In 1998 some of the magic of 1997 seemed to be gone. Martina won titles, and held on to her Number 1 ranking for most of the year. But she lost matches too. She struggled with setbacks.

In January Martina lost to power player Venus Williams in the second round of the singles in the Sydney International in Australia. To be shut out in the second round was a shock. She had beaten Williams before. But there is always another chance in tennis. She rallied to win the doubles title with Sukova.

Martina arrived at the Australian Open, in Melbourne later in January. She faced a lot of expectations. She had won both titles there the year before. She was seeded Number 1 going into the tournament.

"Seeding" is a ranking or standing granted leading tennis players. Being seeded Number 1 means having the highest standing. Tournaments are organized so that highly seeded players do not meet in the early rounds. All eyes are on the highly seeded players to see how they perform.

As the Number 1 seed, the pressure on Martina was high at the Australian Open. She had a cold, and it was hot playing on the outdoor courts. She put out a lot of effort getting through the draw. The third round with Kournikova was not easy. Pierce in the quarterfinal and Anke in the semifinal were both tough opponents. To reach the finals she had to play three sets in the singles and three sets in the doubles on the same day.

She entered the doubles with Mirjana Lucic. They had never played in a tournament together before, but were good friends. Martina enjoyed playing with a friend. Entering as a "wildcard team," unseeded, they defeated the Numbers 1, 2, 8, and 9 seeds during the draw. They seemed to play together better and better as they went on. Martina and Lucic won the doubles title, defeating Lindsay Davenport and Natasha Zvereva in the final.

Still happy from this win, Martina defended her singles title the next day against Conchita Martinez. Martinez hits the ball hard from the baseline and has a strong backhand slice. She wears down her opponents. Beating her requires patience and endurance.

Martina has always found Martinez tough to beat. But she had the patience and kept fighting back, in spite of her cold. She defeated Martinez, 6–3, 6–3. When she won this match, Martina was happier than ever before.

"It was a lot harder than last year because there were so many different expectations of me — pressure — especially from myself," she said. "I really wanted to defend this title. This I'd say was the hardest Grand Slam I had to win, so far, that I won."

It felt great to live up to expectations. She thanked the crowd for being with her through the good and the bad times. This win made her the youngest player to successfully defend a Grand Slam title in the Open Era. She was 17 years, four months and one day old. It was also her fourth Grand Slam singles title. Martina broke a record over 100 years old. She was the youngest in tennis history to defend a major championship, second only to Lottie Dod's defense of Wimbledon in 1888.

Martina was named Chase Monthly Champion for January. The Chase Manhattan Bank donated $1,000 in her name to the World Health Organization's (WHO) immunization program.

During the Australian Open Martina became the youngest player to earn $5 million in career prize money at 17 years, four months. She earned $383,200 for the singles win alone.

The day after her singles win, Martina left for Tokyo, Japan, early in the morning. There was no time to rest before the Pan Pacific Open.

In Tokyo Martina fought hard through the singles draw. She defeated Rita Grande in the quarterfinal.

Facing her good friend Iva Majoli in the semifinal, Martina won 6–0, 6–2. Majoli had defeated Martina in the 1997 French Open final, the only Grand Slam title Martina failed to win that year.

Martina played against Lindsay Davenport of the USA in the final. Davenport hits the ball very hard from the baseline. Her style is a challenge to Martina, and this time the challenge was too much. Davenport won the singles title, but Martina didn't give up the whole tournament to her rival. She and Mirjana Lucic defeated Davenport and Natasha Zvereva to win the doubles competition.

The Pan Pacific Open finished on February 8th. Martina had some time off at home for the rest of February. Then she flew to Indian Wells, California, for the Evert Cup tournament. On March 5th the tournament began.

The rest seemed to make a difference. Martina played strong matches through the whole of the singles draw. She took down player after player in dramatic defeats. She won again over Conchita Martinez in the quarterfinal. Even Venus Williams's power serves couldn't stop her in the semifinal.

Finally Martina won her second singles title of 1998. She turned the tables on Lindsay Davenport, who had just beaten Martina the month before at the Pan Pacific Open. She defeated Davenport, 6–3, 6–4. She lost the doubles this time, though. The tournament ended on March 15.

Only four days later Martina began the Lipton Championships in Key Biscayne, Florida, USA. Martina faced a tough opponent in Serena Williams, Venus's younger sister, in the quarterfinal. Like Venus, Serena has a strong serve and returns the ball hard.

Martina defeated Serena. But she lost the singles semifinal to Venus Williams's fastball, changeup serves, and powerful ground strokes, 2–6, 7–5, 2–6. This was her second loss to Venus in the year. Martina seemed to feel it. She came back to win the doubles title with her usual doubles partner, Jana Novotna. They won over Alexandra Fusai and Nathalie Tauziat.

Martina went on to win another title in Germany. From April 27 to May 3 the International Damen Grand Prix took place in Hamburg. There Martina won her first European clay court singles title. She defeated Jana Novotna in straight sets, 6–3, 7–5. This meant she had won over Novotna on all four surfaces: clay, grass, carpet, and hard. She lost the doubles with Novotna, though, in the final. They were defeated by Barbara Schett and Patty Schnyder.

Right after the German tournament, Martina flew to Rome for the Italian Open. There she defeated Irina Spirlea, Anna Kournikova, and Mirjana Lucic on her way to the final. She faced Venus Williams again. Williams had triumphed at the Lipton. But here Martina won 6–3, 2–6, 6–3. Martina had her second European clay court singles title.

During the Italian Open Martina became the youngest to earn $6 million. She also became the youngest player in the Open Era to win 18 singles titles at 17 years, seven months, 10 days (12 days younger than Tracy Austin).

Martina took no titles at the German Open in Berlin in May. She defeated Majoli in the third round, their first meeting on clay since the 1997 French Open, 6–1, 6–2. But she lost to Anna Kournikova in the quarterfinal of the singles. She didn't seem to have her usual concentration. She said, "I could have lost to anyone that day. I didn't care if I won or lost. You can't win every match."

Where was her usual competitive edge? Martina had always cared before. She always wanted to win. Was she just tired from the heavy schedule? Was she having teenage growing pains? Some suggest she was in a bad mood. Maybe her relationship with her boyfriend, Julian Alonso, wasn't going well. She had met the Spanish ATP player at the '98 Australian Open. Their relationship ended in the fall of 1998. Martina's ups and downs during '98 seemed to be influenced by her relationship with Julian.

Whatever the reason, Martina's mind seemed to be on other things, not on tennis, in the 1998 season. Losses were piling up.

Later in May Martina arrived at the French Open in Paris. This was the only Grand Slam she failed to win in 1997. And she did not go into the Open from a string of victories. She was less confident. Martina was clearly struggling during her last two singles matches. She won over Venus Williams in the quarterfinals, but not easily. Four times Martina appealed a line call, questioning whether the line umpire had correctly called the ball in or out of the court.

Martina went on a date the night before her semifinal against Monica Seles. She joked around on the practice court the next day. She didn't seem to take the practice seriously. Her boyfriend Julian went back to Spain before the match. Martina seemed down.

Monica Seles, one of the past greats, was trying for a comeback. The year before, Martina had defeated Seles at the French Open. Six times Martina had defeated Seles. But Seles had gained strength and concentration in the past year.

In the semifinal, Martina lost badly to Seles. "It certainly wasn't my best effort," Martina admitted. "I knew right from the beginning that it was not going to be my day." Martina seemed distracted. Sanchez Vicario took the singles title from Seles in the end. But Martina was already out of play.

Chris Evert counsels Martina as part of the Corel WTA Tour mentor program. In her time she had been a tennis teen queen, too. She came of age in the public eye. It's a difficult road. Evert lost matches, too, and emotions played their part. She had some bad days, but she turned it around. Can Martina?

Martina was Chase Monthly Champion for May, in spite of losses. The Chase Manhattan Bank donated another $1,000 in her name to WHO's immunization program.

In June Martina travelled to London, England, where she had won the year before. The Wimbledon Championships began on June 22. Martina didn't even make it to the finals. She lost the singles title to Jana Novotna. Novotna defeated Nathalie Tauziat in the final. Martina teamed with Novotna again in doubles. There she fared better — she and Novotna won the doubles title over Lindsay Davenport and Natasha Zvereva.

Martina lost at the Bank of the West Classic in Stanford, USA, in July and then the Toshiba Tennis Classic in San Diego, USA, in August. Lindsay Davenport was the singles winner at both. At the Acura Classic in Manhattan Beach, USA, later in August, Martina fared better, defeating Arantxa Sanchez Vicario in the semifinals. Then she faced Lindsay Davenport in the finals.

Playing what reporters call "big girl tennis," Davenport displayed strong form. She hit the ball very hard from the baseline and returned balls from the corners on the run, using her long reach. Perhaps most decisive, her serves were powerful.

Martina took more risks than usual in response. She made many more errors. Her shots went wild.

When Davenport took the singles title in the final, 4–6, 6–4, 6–3, Martina tossed her racket in disgust. In Davenport, Martina may have met her match.

"When you're No. 1 for as long as I have been, there always is someone out there who is motivated to try to beat you. I don't think I've gotten any worse, but the other girls have become much better," Martina said shortly afterward.

In mid-August, Martina began the du Maurier Open in Montreal, Canada, strongly, winning her first victory in straight sets. She had switched to a shorter, titanium-based racket. It took her almost two hours to defeat Sandrine Testud in the quarterfinals. Characteristically, she embraced her opponent and complimented her on her game. She even laughed when a reporter called her Monica by mistake.

But after winning the first set 6–4 against Seles in the semifinals, Martina was overpowered. She lost in three sets, failing to reach the finals. Seles took the singles title over Sanchez Vicario.

Ever ready to try again, Martina paired with Jana Novotna to win the doubles title at the du Maurier.

"Last year it was my goal to be Number 1 in singles and this year, I'm trying to be Number 1 in doubles, too," she told Rosie DiManno of the *Toronto Star*. "When you lose in singles, it always puts you in a better mood when you win the doubles. And it would be nice to win a Grand Slam in something ... I've got three Grand Slam titles and the fourth is coming up."

Her prediction came true at the US Open in early September in New York. Again she got in some impressive wins. Perhaps most significant was a strong singles victory over Monica Seles, in quick revenge for the du Maurier, on the way to the semifinals. Martina took Seles in straight sets, 6–4, 6–4, in nearly perfect form, in a windy open-air match. Seles called Martina very quick. "I don't think people give her enough credit," Seles said.

In the semifinals, Martina beat third-seeded Jana Novotna, coming from behind in the third set. But in the finals her new nemesis, Lindsay Davenport, put Martina on the defensive with serves over 100 miles (160 kilometres) per hour, and strong ground strokes. Davenport took the title in straight sets, 6–3, 7–5. Martina seemed to be overpowered. But not so in the doubles: Martina and Novotna defeated Davenport and Natasha Zvereva solidly in two sets, 6–3, 6–3.

This gave Martina her Grand Slam in the doubles — Australian Open, French Open, Wimbledon, and US Open. Martina was saying to the world, "I'm not out of the running yet," in a powerful way.

At the Fed Cup in Geneva, Switzerland, in September, Martina posted solid wins over Conchita Martinez and Arantxa Sanchez Vicario. It looked as though she would lead Switzerland to victory over Spain, but two losses by Patty Schnyder of Switzerland led to a tie, and a loss in the tie-breaking doubles put Spain in the winner's circle.

A new tournament for women, the Grand Slam Cup in Munich, Germany, brings together the players with the best records in the Grand Slam events of the year. Martina opened by beating Martinez 6–2, 7–5, in an erratic match. This gave her six wins over Martinez in their eight career encounters. At first leading 5–1 against Patty Schnyder, Martina retired at 5–5 in the third set. Apparently Martina was bothered by cramps. Venus Williams overpowered Schnyder to win the Cup.

During the Porsche Grand Prix at Filderstadt, Germany, the tide seemed to change. Martina prevailed against Anna Kournikova in three sets, but, slowed by an ankle injury, lost to Dominique Van Roost in a two-hour, 18-minute quarterfinal battle.

On October 9, 1998, Martina slipped to Number 2 in the ratings, as Davenport passed her by. Martina had held Number 1 for 80 weeks, taking over from Steffi Graf. Her 1998 record stood at 54–10, including three losses to Davenport. Martina took the news with grace.

"It's no drama that I'll be the No. 2 for a little while. It's good for the motivation," said Martina. "But at the moment, Lindsay is simply the better player. She belongs at No. 1."

Small injuries and setbacks had added up. Martina admitted she was thinking of taking a break, but showed she would not be content to stay Number 2 for long.

Can Martina regain her winning form? The answer may depend on how well can she handle defeats. Her attitude is still positive. She admits it when she hasn't played well, but she works on improving.

"I'm definitely not as confident as last year or at the other tournaments at the beginning of this year," Martina told writer Tom Tebbit in the fall of 1998. "You even think you can't lose to anybody. Then all of a sudden it can happen in the Grand Slams. I wouldn't lose to a nobody, but I lost to Monica [Seles] and Jana [Novotna] and they're great players. So far I haven't lost to anyone who isn't Top 10. You just want to hang in there and try to be better again."

Can she concentrate on tennis the way she did in 1997? "You have other things on your mind once you get older," she commented. "Probably you want to just hang out and go out with friends." These are the words of a teenager, perhaps simply acting her age.

Despite her recent setbacks, Martina is staying in the game. She grows stronger as she matures. The women's tennis field is wide open and full of talented players with widely varying styles. Each of the Grand Slams in 1998 was won by a different player. As the world's attention is on her, Martina will prove in 1999 and beyond whether her best tennis is still ahead of her.

# Chapter 8

# Life in the Spotlight

What is it like to be a teenager at the top of the high-powered tennis world?

"It's just unbelievable," Martina exclaimed when asked about her success. "It's a little dream come true. Every time you go out people are shouting, 'Hey, Martina,' and they want to give you things. You get dinner for free sometimes. I even got to meet Sylvester Stallone."

Martina is excited. She revels in the spotlight. She loves the recognition, the adulation, and the freedom of her jet-set life. She has money and privileges.

Yet she doesn't like to trade on her rank for favors. And she hasn't forgotten what it was like to idolize the top players. Martina admired Monica Seles when she was a child. Martina even got Seles's autograph at a tournament in Europe.

Later she played against, and ultimately defeated Seles. Such successes would go to most teenagers' heads. They might become proud or distant. Martina has become neither.

She's gracious when approached by fans or reporters. At the 1996 American Cup a small boy, perhaps six years of age, walked down from the cheapest seats in the house, leaned over the railing, and called to Martina, asking for an autograph. She smiled radiantly and walked over to give him the autograph.

Even with all the attention, Martina has a sense of perspective. Chris Evert noticed that Martina always asked to see the pictures of Evert's sons. Upon seeing them, Martina responded, "This is what it's all about, isn't it?" Martina seems mature enough to know that the most important things in life aren't ratings or fame.

What do people notice first about Martina? Her ready laugh and radiant smile. She charms audiences by showing what she feels during a match. Other tennis teen queens might be grim and business-like on the court. They might be more like competitive machines than girls. Not Martina. She smiles and laughs during play. If she's frustrated she shows that too. She threw her racket across the court during the 1997 French Open. She is learning to control her temper and respond more graciously in losses. But she has still remained natural.

Some tennis stars become impatient with reporters. The questions never seem to stop. Martina is pleasant during interviews. How can she stay so natural?

"Tennis is not my life. I would get bored very soon if I would think just about tennis," Martina says. It's important to her to do other things, just for fun. She tries to have a well-rounded life, in spite of a packed schedule.

In many ways, she is normal. During the 1997 Australian Open, she went to the theater; during the French Open, to the Louvre museum and Notre Dame cathedral; during the US Open, on shopping expeditions to posh stores like Saks and Donna Karan. After the Lipton Championships, Martina hit the boutiques in Miami's Coconut Grove. She's always on the lookout for a new dress to wear to a tournament party.

Martina roots for the Chicago Bulls at basketball games. She enjoys Bulls star Dennis Rodman's antics and dyed hair. Martina still takes time for other sports, especially horseback riding (though not jumping, following her injury) and in-line skating.

She has a passion for food and can put on a bit of weight during the winter. She seeks out spicy foods like chicken fajitas, but also likes sushi. Martina loves Haagen-Dazs strawberry ice cream. She definitely has a sweet tooth. In 1998 she cut out candy, pizza, and sugared fruit drinks in order to squeeze into her new wardrobe of tight dresses and short skirts.

But tennis takes up most of Martina's time and energy. It has to, if you want to be the best, and Martina has had that goal all her life. She absorbed the goal from her mother and made it her own, but it doesn't own her.

The money doesn't seem to dominate her either, though she is building a house in Roznov, her mother's hometown, and another for her father in Slovakia. "Life doesn't change because you just won $100,000," she said in 1997. "I still can't drive a car, I still can't go out, because I'm under age everywhere." This echoes the moans of teens everywhere. She wants the freedoms that will come with getting older, and she wants them now.

If you want to know if Martina is a real teenager, look at her hair. She has streaked her hair blue and purple, and dyed it black. She has started wearing makeup and nail polish. Her new clothes choices tell it all. Gone are the sweats. Now she likes to wear black, with lace.

Martina also has superstitions. She never steps on the lines of the court. She uses the same shower and toilet in a locker room. She even carries a miniature Swiss cowbell in her racket bag.

Teenager or jet-setter, what kind of a person is Martina Hingis?

Someone once suggested that Martina became Number 1 only because Steffi Graf, the former Number 1, was injured. Martina replied that Graf's injury wasn't her problem. At the 1997 Australian Open, after winning the singles and the doubles, Martina joked that she wouldn't enter the mixed doubles because she wanted someone else to have a chance to win. Asked about her 1997 "rivalry" with Russian Anna Kournikova, she said, "I don't think it's such a big rivalry — I always beat her."

These comments have made some think Martina is arrogant. Yet Martina delivers these lines with a look of innocence or a smile. She seems merely blunt, honest, or tactless. Some say she has the Swiss forthrightness, simply stating what she believes to be true.

Her confidence can be jarring. During her 1997 run of wins, when asked if she was unbeatable, she replied that she was, for now. Incredibly, such comments haven't put off her peers. She is well liked in the locker room. She has made friends among her fellow players, such as Iva Majoli.

"I like her cockiness and self-belief," said Billie Jean King. "She's not a passive woman. She's saying, 'I'm here, and I'm really good, and I like being here. Watch me!'...We've felt for two or three years that she's the best in the world."

After a string of losses in 1998, Martina was much less cocky. She admitted she had lost concentration during some matches. Sometimes discouraged, she returned again and again to the courts. Over-confidence may have undermined her. After losing so many titles, lack of confidence might become a problem. But Martina showed determination. She seemed to tell herself to snap out of it. She fought back, against players bigger and more powerful than she. Then she began winning again. Her talent and her strengths came forward. Her unique gifts continue to bring trophies.

Martina respects other players. She'll say so when someone has played a good game against her, win or lose. She admits making mistakes too. Her honesty applies to herself.

Martina's bold confidence and willingness to take chances helped her climb to the top. She didn't wear a helmet when horseback riding and jumping, until her spills led to surgery. Fearlessness can be dangerous, too. Now she wears a helmet. She still rides her horses and in-line skates before big tournaments. Taking chances is part of her personality. Many tennis players retire in their twenties because of injuries. Maybe Martina has learned this now. But she hasn't stopped doing the things that give her joy. All the signs are that she couldn't. Her zest for life fuels the energy we see on the court.

In 1998 teenage mood swings hit her hard. "I hate my age," she said. "Lately, I get moody and behave like a 13-year-old for no reason. I just learned the word 'funk' because I'm often in one these days." These moods seem to be the reasons for some defeats. Her concentration, her whole heart hasn't been in some of her matches. At the top, competing against the toughest and the best, there is no room for moods.

Martina isn't as single-minded as other teens who made it to the top — Tracy Austin, Steffi Graf, Monica Seles. When Graf and Seles were teens, they were controlled strictly by their father-coaches. They kept their focus. Martina is a different kind of person. Her mental game and her all-round strengths took her to the top. Are they enough? Martina is sometimes lazy. She doesn't like to practice. Molitor has helped her overcome these problems.

"[My mother] always knows what to do. If she wasn't there, I probably would not do all the practices and probably would party a little bit more. But we have made rules. She makes sure I do the right things and keep going." They are a team. They debate the training routine. Sometimes Molitor will lay down the law, but she is not a dictator.

Who is Martina? She's a young woman who loves tennis but won't sacrifice everything to the game. She's outgoing, with an easy-going approach, and yet a competitive passion. She made friends and kept her poise at the top.

What does a typical day for Martina look like? She spends 35 weeks of the year on tour. During those weeks she plays about 20 tournaments and two Federation Cups. So "typical" covers a lot of ground. A lot of her nights are spent away from home in hotel rooms. She is often aboard a jet plane, on her way to the next tournament. She spends a lot of time playing in matches, or waiting in players' lounges.

Every tournament is a series of grueling contests. Martina must win over and over in order to reach the finals. And she plays against the best. Every player presents her with a new challenge. She must change her strategy every time, yet still be fresh.

Martina has tremendous energy. Her outlook is positive. She celebrates every victory. But even she can get tired and stressed. After a day full of tough games she sometimes has trouble sleeping. She sometimes awakens in the night. After a night of broken sleep, she must rise early again. She has to get out and practice again to stay in peak form. Then she has to give all of her attention and energy to another match. It would wear down anyone. Years of training help her continue this punishing schedule. The routine her mother has established for her is her foundation stone.

At 8:00 a.m. Martina will have breakfast, usually cereal or toast. After that she will practice tennis for about 2 1/2 hours, under her mother's direction. This will usually include time with a male partner. (All the best women players use male partners who can handle their power.) Peter Holik, two years older than Martina, is her longtime training partner. Says Holik, "When Martina was 8, she was already without competition. She played against 16-year-olds, and she wiped them out."

Lunch will be a sandwich and fruit, perhaps. In the afternoon, if Martina is not playing a tournament she participates in other sports and athletic activities — hiking, biking, jogging, basketball, or soccer with other young people, skiing, swimming, in-line skating (she takes her skates with her on tour). Boxing and weight lifting were added recently as cross-training exercises.

Martina goes horseback riding one hour a day, whenever possible. One of the greatest thrills in her life was buying her first horse. She now owns two horses — Montana and Sorrenta. She takes riding gear with her on tour, and finds a mount when she can. At home she'll disappear by herself into the mountains nearby, riding. She loves the mountains and the town where she lives in a modest house. There she plays with her dog, a German shepherd called Zorro, skis, and enjoys her privacy.

When Martina is at home in Trubbach a physiotherapist visits regularly, and she gets massages. She loves the massages especially. They leave her feeling completely relaxed, like jelly.

Home schooling has to fit in too. Martina quit regular school when she turned pro at the age of 14. Now she has a private tutor.

Dinner is usually with her mother. Martina calls Molitor her best friend. Sometimes she will eat with friends. Her favorite food for this meal is sushi or chicken.

Her closest friends are other tennis players. She has often beaten them or played with them. They include 20-year-old Iva Majoli of Croatia, Anke Huber, age 23, of Germany, and Mirjana Lucic, age 15, of Croatia. During tournaments they go to parties together.

Outings, when she can fit them in, include shopping for clothes and presents, visits to the theater, and sightseeing. She goes with her mother or friends. After a busy day Martina often watches television before collapsing into bed. Her favorite show is *The X-Files.* She also watches basketball and soccer. She admires Alpine ski racer Alberto Tomba of Italy, horseback rider Franke Sloothak, and her WTA mentor, Chris Evert.

Music is important to her, too. She has a collection of over 300 CDs. She spends time listening to her favorite musicians — Celine Dion, Jon Bon Jovi, Whitney Houston, and Alanis Morissette. And Martina enjoys movies. She liked *Forrest Gump, Free Willy,* and *The Man from Snowy River.* Tom Hanks and Julia Roberts are actors she loves to watch. *Miss Saigon* is her favorite musical.

She used to go to bed at 10:00 p.m. An athlete in training needs a lot of sleep, and so does a growing adolescent. In 1998 her curfew was extended to 11:00 p.m., after she began to date.

During matches Martina gets up early and practices. Every time she goes out onto the court, she is tested. It's very hard to be at her best, day after day. After each match she meets with reporters. Before a match she eats pasta or fruit, to give her energy.

Does she like her life? "I think there are many more things about it which are positive than negative. I mean I went to the mall this morning ... and there are always people coming up to me and they congratulate me, and I went to a watch store, and just everybody recognized me, and you get things for free you wouldn't get if you wouldn't be so famous, so that's nice about it. Or I get so many chances to see so many different people. I get to see basketball or whatever I want. So I really like this life. I have to say that."

## Chapter 9

# The Business of Being a Star

Once tennis was a game. Now it's a multi-million-dollar business. The business is jack-hammer driven by television. Regency Productions made the very successful movies *J.F.K.* and *L.A. Confidential.* Regency has bought the television rights to the WTA Tour. The contract is for five years, and may be renewed for another four years. The deal is worth perhaps $200 million. IMG used to hold the television rights, for perhaps $5 million a year.

Stars like Martina are the reason so much money is at stake. Her battles with other tennis teen queens and veterans have made tennis exciting. To movie moguls, she is one of the gladiators. To the public, she is fascinating. Once a few people could get tickets to see their favorite tennis star. Now millions can see Martina on television, in over 100 countries in the world.

It's not just television that makes tennis big. Constant newspaper and magazine articles appear. And now, in the electronic age, Martina is an Internet happening too. There is late-breaking Web news. There are advertising blitzes. There are celebrity-linked products to buy.

Martina smashed so many records that she amazed us all. She became the best at her sport at such a young age. With her winning personality, she charmed us. She is attractive, with a dazzling smile, a healthy lifestyle, and a fun-loving nature. Well spoken, she is at ease in front of the camera, and disarmingly frank with reporters. Her zest for life shows. She is perfect star material — a young innocent with talent and high spirits, in the top ranks of her sport.

Across the world her name is known, her career is followed. She has star power. As millions of people watch her matches on television, they watch the commercials that go with them. Companies pay large sums of money to advertise on these shows. If Martina wears a certain watch, people notice and want to buy the same kind of watch. When she signs a contract to use a product, or have her photograph or name appear in ads, that is called an endorsement. In some contracts Martina has promised to appear on television ads, attend promotional functions and have her name and picture used in magazines or on the Internet.

In all these ways, Martina earns additional income. Martina is a millionaire many times over. Her business dealings are handled by the International Management Group. When she was 12 years old they noticed her and arranged a five-year contract. Her latest contract is for 13 years, estimated at $2 million per year.

Martina has wide appeal to advertisers because her interests include so many sports, including horseback riding and skiing. In business terms, that means she appeals to a wide market base.

Sergio Tacchini is a clothing and footwear company. Martina first signed a contract with them when she was 14. She had just become the junior Wimbledon champion. Her latest deal with them is worth $10 million. She wears the Tacchini sport shoes Satisfaction.

Ocean Spray Cranberries Inc., a manufacturer of fruit drinks, has signed Martina as their three-year spokesperson for around a half-million dollars. They plan to feature her in print and TV ads for their new "Ruby Red & Mango" grapefruit juice drink. Martina has also agreed to make personal appearances. The company wants to appeal to young women.

Opel, the German car manufacturer, signed a three-year sponsorship deal with Martina in February 1997 for about $2 million per year. Opel would not reveal the exact figures.

Omega, makers of Swiss watches, is paying Martina an estimated $750,000 per year for the use of her name and picture. Their ads even appear on the Internet, and she wears their watches.

Martina was linked to Glico brand powdered milk in Japan early in her career. In Japan, she is a megastar. The powdered milk comes in cans and is very popular.

The Bolle company makes sunglasses, goggles, and other eyewear. Their eyewear is used for sports and for safety. They signed a multi-year contract with Martina in December 1997. Martina agreed to wear only Bolle sunglasses, sport glasses and ski goggles at all public events and even when she's playing for fun. She will also appear in Bolle ads, and in promotions around the world.

Also under contract to Bolle is 1997 World Champion Formula One driver Jacques Villeneuve. There was speculation about a possible relationship between the two after they appeared in an ad together, and were seen chatting. Martina dismissed the rumors with a laugh, saying they were just friends. This kind of rumor is part of the price of fame.

Clairol is slated to use Martina to promote a shampoo, most likely its Herbal Essences brand, in late spring of 1999.

Yonex has been supplying her tennis rackets for years. She played with a Yonex Super RD Tour 95, and a Yonex Pro RD-70 Long. An Italian mineral water company has also made a deal with Martina. She represents Limpia Pellegrino.

The money keeps rolling in. What does she do with it? Besides building houses, she spends money on clothes, dinners, and movies. Her horses are costly to maintain. But mostly, the money gets put in the bank.

In exchange for the money she earns from her advertising work and tennis wins, Martina has had to give up some things. Being a star means losing a lot of privacy. Martina is recognized all over the world. She cannot go anywhere without being greeted by strangers. Reporters request numerous interviews. Her mother has set limits to these interviews.

She has fan clubs all over the world. Her agent helps her deal with fan mail and send out pictures. Martina cannot answer the thousands of requests herself.

On the Internet she's called a goddess, and shrines are dedicated to her honor. Hundreds of thousands of fans visit Web sites to know every detail of her wins, losses, life, and loves. Every scrap of news, public or personal, is sent across the globe in seconds — her favorite foods, colors, movies, musicians, television shows, horses, her latest dates. There was even a worldwide auction of her original tournament clothing on the Internet.

Like any star, Martina is asked to appear to publicize causes. To promote the Chase Championships she played table tennis with customers at the Official All-Star Cafe in New York.

How has Martina responded to fame? From the beginning she loved to be recognized, to get good seats at the NBA games, to receive gifts. But what of the future?

Already she says she feels better when she's back home in Trubbach, where people don't bother her, or ask for her autograph (because most of them have it already).

There is another down side to fame. Some fans go too far. They follow their idols endlessly, trying to get too close. At least once this has happened to Martina. On January 25, 1998, Australian Open officials banned a fan who had pursued Martina. Security guards were ordered to restrain the fan and more guards were posted at the matches. People getting near the players were watched closely. Monica Seles was stabbed while she sat courtside in 1993. Since then the dangers of fame are more noticed in tennis circles. Like other stars, top tennis players can be targets for disturbed people.

Despite these worries, Martina seems to realize how lucky she is compared to many in the world. Martina doesn't just bank or spend her money. She gives it to good causes too, following the example of the Chase Manhattan Bank. The bank donated $3,000 in her name to the World Health Organization (WHO) in 1997. (Martina was overall Chase Champion of that year for 1997 with 75 singles wins.)

In October 1997 she donated over $80,000 to the WHO to further their vaccination program. She earned most of this money during the 1997 Arthur Ashe Kids' Day before the US Open, then added her own money. The WHO is trying to get rid of polio in Ethiopia, and neonatal tetanus in Nepal. This kind of tetanus attacks the unborn children of pregnant women, and can be fatal. "Millions of children die every year and even if it is impossible for me to alter this sad situation, I want to send out a message: vaccination can prevent these deaths," Martina said.

When Martina became interested in these programs she wanted to do more than just give money. She agreed to act as a "roving ambassador" for the WHO to help promote their vaccination program. In February 1998, she visited Nepal, where she was welcomed by a cheering crowd. She visited three immunization centers, including a primary health care center, a school, and a health post. The Nepalese people hung garlands of flowers around her neck to show their affection and gratitude.

The program was very large. More than 12,000 women were immunized against tetanus in May 1997. "The craziest thing I saw was when I visited a village where tetanus shots were being given to 13-, 14-year-old girls so their children would be born healthy," said Martina. "It was incredible to see girls younger than me who were pregnant, and some had a child already."

As of August 1998, Martina's career prizes topped $6.7 million. Add the millions in endorsements, and you get an idea of her wealth. Friends say it hasn't changed her, though. She's still a teenager who loves to play tennis and have fun.

# Chapter 10

# The Impact of the Phenom

What effect has Martina had on the tennis world? "The more she keeps winning, the more impact she'll have," says Navratilova. But she has already made her mark.

A few decades ago, exciting, talented players like Martina Navratilova, Billie Jean King, and Chris Evert made women's tennis worth watching. They played brilliantly, with differing styles. No one knew which of them would take the title. Even when Navratilova stayed at the top, the others gave her real competition.

Finally, this group of players retired. Stars like Monica Seles and Steffi Graf brought a lot of power to the game, but less interest. They slugged it out on the court in grim, grunting battles. And they dominated. There wasn't much suspense about who was going to win. They had injuries and other problems off the court. People began to tune out tennis.

Martina and other teen tennis players have brought new excitement to the tennis world. "They strut, they squabble, they pose for fashion spreads.

They're also great for the game,"opined a writer for *Newsweek* magazine. Martina belongs to a feisty, bold new generation of players. They aren't afraid to argue about line calls. Martina has stopped a match for a bathroom break. Venus Williams changed clothes part way through a match. Were these really tactics to break their opponents' focus?

Martina was the first female athlete covergirl of the popular men's magazine *GQ* in June 1998. She didn't appear in tennis togs. Instead she wore a clinging, shoulderless dress cut away at the hips. She showed some glamour. Was this the same girl who tosses her racket in disgust on the court? Yes, and the world loves the contrast.

There's no doubt about it. Martina and the other teen queens of tennis have attracted a lot of attention. More people watched the US Open final between Martina and Venus Williams on television in 1997 than watched the men's final.

What does the future hold for Martina? "I would like to prove that I am not a flash in the pan," Martina says. "The better you are, the less you want to lose."

And she definitely doesn't want to lose. The world of professional tennis is tough and competitive. Martina has to face many kinds of players — experienced players, like Novotna and Sanchez Vicario, strong players trying to come back, like Monica Seles and Steffi Graf, talented teens like Kournikova and the

Williams sisters, and players just maturing, led by Lindsay Davenport. Martina is highly gifted, but does she have the necessary power and aggression? Can she focus when she needs to? Can she regain her standing?

Some speculated in 1996 that she may have more personality than drive and more talent than discipline. As Swiss journalist Heinz Mazenauer said, "I don't know if she has that killer instinct that top champions have. At this stage, she's the kind of player who plays well when she feels like it, when she is in a good mood. I'm not sure how far that can take a player in today's game."

Going through teenage changes in public isn't easy. The trials of the teen years seem to have affected Martina's game. Can she grow into, rather than out of the game? Her mother and coach seems to think so. Molitor says, "It's a difficult time, but ... we still have many years of tennis ahead of us."

Martina is having an impact on how tennis is being played, too. She's swinging the game more toward tactics. Who will rule tennis in the next few years — the power players or Martina?

"It's all about her head," tennis player Tracy Austin commented to *Tennis* magazine in 1998. "That's what makes Martina head over heels better than everybody else. She has the diversity, she can change the game, she can hit soft and hard, but mostly she knows how and when to use what strokes. She's bringing tennis back to strategy, getting back to the guts of the game."

Tennis styles have changed with the times. Games based on tactics have been played less in the past 10 years. Power players took over for a while. Navratilova won her last Grand Slam singles titles in 1987 (Wimbledon and US Open) and 1990 (Wimbledon). Steffi Graf won her first Grand Slam title in 1987 (French Open). Monica Seles, another power player, came on the scene about the same time. Their styles had an impact.

"Steffi and Monica — that's the power period," says Chris Evert, whose 18 Grand Slam singles titles stretch from 1974 to 1986. "Those two learned from a young age how to crunch the balls with those graphite rackets and still maintain control. It's safe to say that Martina [Navratilova] and I had better feel, touch and finesse, but Steffi and Monica had the power over us."

Why the change? It wasn't just the players. The rackets made a difference too. The new rackets have frames made of fiberglass and graphite, not wood. They're light, and they give more power to the ball. Tactics are less important when the balls travel so fast. Older players had trouble adjusting to the new rackets. Young players, who learned on them, are changing the game even more.

Experience still counts. It takes years to develop really great serves and volleys. Graf prevented younger players from moving up for a while. Then Martina came along. She didn't rely on power; she had other gifts. Now she in turn is being challenged by power players.

"They try to hit the ball very hard. Everything is fast. But I never tried to hit the ball as hard as I could because I was always the younger one. I just never had the power of a Mary Pierce or Steffi Graf," says Martina. So she developed an all-round game, using every shot. She became very quick and cunning. And she won over bigger, stronger, older girls.

Other players show they can use tactics. Jana Novotna's game reduces the power of her opponents. She won the 1997 Chase Championships this way. Sanchez Vicario and Martinez play with old-school tactics, too, but Martina has beaten them.

Venus Williams is a power player. Her serves can travel up to 122 miles (196 kilometres) per hour. Such a serve can be crushing. But Williams can also make deep ground strokes and shots with a softer touch. She is trying to vary her game, to learn all the shots on the court. Why? Maybe power isn't enough to win by itself anymore. Or is it?

Nick Bollettieri, the renowned Florida tennis coach who runs the top-notch Bollettieri Sports Academy and has trained Pierce, Seles, and Majoli, warns, "Don't say the power game is extinct yet. Power players can still power you off the court." About Venus Williams and her younger sister Serena, whom he is training, he says, "They're sheer power ... They're going to beat you up."

Martina's most important loss in 1997 was to Iva Majoli. Majoli delivered very hard ground strokes in the French Open final. They were too much for Martina. Then Martina lost to Mary Pierce, another power player, in the Chase Championships. Pierce is one of the best strong baseliners. In the 1998 US Open, Lindsay Davenport bested Martina with an aggressive power game. So Martina can be overpowered sometimes by the best.

Evert disagrees. "The new generation always finds an answer, always figures out a way to beat the old guard," she told *Tennis* magazine. "It's obvious that power tennis isn't necessarily the way to go now. With the power, we lost the thinking, the finesse and drop shots. Now, as long as players emulate the No. 1, as they always seem to do, we can expect to see more of it back. It's the wave of the future: Hit hard, then let up."

Martina is still far from finished. She'll get over the normal teenage distractions. We'll probably see her at her full powers when she is in her 20s. That's when a well-trained tennis player peaks, as long as she can avoid serious injuries. And her training is aimed at long-term success, not instant stardom.

"So what if Martina blows a few matches?" Evert says. "She'll get through it and learn how to focus, just as I did." Martina shows more patience in the ups and downs than most teens. When she loses a tournament, she goes on to try harder in the next.

"Martina needs to work harder and get into better shape," Molitor says. "She doesn't need to practice more hours, but has to concentrate better on court." Molitor doesn't sound worried. "She has ups and downs like most 17-year-olds. Every year, there are different things to deal with. Last year, it was the knee injury. Now, she is becoming a grown woman who is learning what is important."

Always, Molitor is a loving mother first, and a coach second. She is most proud of the caring, level-headed young woman Martina has become. They still show affection for each other. And they work for the future.

As Martina says, "Wait until you see what I'm going to do next."

# Some of the Competition

## Lindsay Davenport, b. USA, 1976

Davenport is the highest ranked American-born woman tennis player since Chris Evert. Since turning pro in 1993, that year's *Tennis* magazine Rookie of the Year, she has quietly climbed the ratings.

Neither a teen queen nor a veteran, often she has been overlooked. Flashier players took the limelight while she steadily won millions in prize money, getting ever closer to the big titles. Meanwhile, she has been working hard to achieve over 100-mph (160-km/h) serves and superb fitness.

Her first Grand Slam title was the doubles in 1996 at Roland Garros. The same year she won singles at the Olympics, Strasbourg, and Los Angeles. In 1997 she took six titles and began to gain confidence. She lost weight and increased her fitness.

In 1998 Davenport came into her own. She toppled Martina Hingis in the 1998 Pan Pacific, the Evert Cup, the Acura Classic, and the US Open — her proudest victory. She became the first American-born woman to win the US Open since Chris Evert in 1982.

Though Martina defeated her in the Evert Cup, Davenport won the Bank of the West Classic over

Venus Williams, and the Toshiba Classic over Mary Pierce. She's also won four doubles titles.

At six feet, two inches (1.88 metres) and 175 pounds (79.5 kilograms), Davenport has power, strength and an impressive reach. Acing many of her serves in the US Open, Davenport put Martina on the defensive. She out-returned Martina, playing aggressively. The modest Davenport has matured and gained confidence steadily through her career. She has proven to be a tough adversary.

Finally, on October 9, 1998, Davenport passed Martina in the rankings to take the No. 1 place. This may be the beginning of a serious rivalry, such as we saw between Navratilova and Evert.

## Steffi Graf, b. Germany, 1969

Graf has been called the greatest player (along with Martina Navratilova) produced in Europe since the 1920s. She possessed both power and speed. Graf turned pro at the age of 13 in 1982.

Her father raised her to play tennis, as Molitor raised Martina. But Graf's father was arrested and imprisoned in 1995 for tax evasion. He was convicted of mismanagement of her money and sentenced in 1997.

Winning 22 major titles in her career, Graf was named World Champion seven times, including 1995 and 1996, and spent a record 374 weeks ranked Number 1.

In recent years she has struggled with back and knee injuries, yet beat Martina twice at Wimbledon. Knee problems caused her to withdraw from the 1997 Pan Pacific, leaving Martina holding the title.

Some believe Graf's career at the top is over, that her age and injuries have caught up with her. Her attempts at a comeback in 1998 were inconclusive, though she made the final of the French Open. She may yet regain her former power.

## Monica Seles, b. Yugoslavia, 1973,
## (US citizen)

Seles was a teen prodigy, too. She was only 15 years old when she defeated Chris Evert, in Evert's last final, in 1989. Nearly six feet tall (1.83 m), Seles had great strength. She was soon piling up titles, slamming the ball back from any part of the court with immense power. She played two-handed backhands, both handed from both sides. She climbed to Number 1 in the rankings by 1991. By mid-1993 she had won eight Grand Slams.

Then, in Hamburg, a German spectator stabbed her in the back while she sat beside the court. Twenty-eight months later she returned to the court, but not to her previous form. Injuries and personal tragedies plagued her. (In 1998 her father died after a five-year fight with stomach cancer.) In 1995 Seles returned to tennis, slowly climbing back toward greatness, though she is old enough to be called a "dowager" in tennis terms.

In 1997 alone, Seles contested with Martina three times in finals, at the Lipton Championships, in the Family Circle Cup, and at the Toshiba Classic. (Martina won all three.) Seles lost to Martina in the semifinals of both the 1997 and 1998 French Open. (Martina lost both opens).

In 1998 Seles surprised everyone. She made it to the final of the French Open, losing to Sanchez Vicario, then won her fourth du Maurier Open. In the 1998 US Open Seles advanced to the quarterfinals where she lost to Martina. Has she recovered her power? She is still a contender.

## Arantxa Sanchez Vicario, b. Spain, 1971

Sanchez Vicario became the youngest winner of the French Open in 1989. She competed well in three Olympics and had won 11 major titles by 1996.

People thought she might have burned out. She suffered wrist and thigh injuries following a win at the 1998 Sydney International. Then she defeated Seles to win the 1998 French Open, after Martina had fallen to Seles. Her style of play is dogged, but determined. Sanchez Vicario can't be counted out of the running yet.

### Jana Novotna, b. Czechoslovakia, 1968

At age 29, Jana Novotna became the oldest Grand Slam singles champion in the Open Era when she won the Wimbledon title in 1998. Novotna was the first Czech to win Wimbledon since Navratilova. (Though born in Czechoslovakia, Martina is now a Swiss national.)

Novotna has choked badly in some matches, as in the long-fought 1993 Wimbledon, when she lost to Steffi Graf. She gave up the 1997 Wimbledon to Martina.

But Novotna has persevered. Though sometimes inconsistent, she is a serve-and-volley player with a strong all-round game. In the 1990s she climbed in the ratings, breaking into the Top Ten and advancing. In July '98 she took second place briefly, to be displaced by Davenport in August. She has logged hundreds of career wins, and made more than $6 million in prize money.

Novotna personifies the threat that experience and years of hard work can bring to the court. Very fit, Novotna is a versatile veteran who can topple tennis giants.

### Venus Williams, b. USA, 1980

One of the teen phenoms, with her sizzling serves and 6 foot-1$^1$/2 inch (1.88 m) height, Williams is a power player, working to round out her game. Strength gives her an edge. Martina can approach the 100-mile-per-hour (160 kilometre-per-hour) serve, but Williams can frequently deliver serves of up to 122 mph (196 km/h). Williams's ground strokes can be searing too. At the 1998 Lipton, they were enough to power Martina off the court.

So far, Williams needs more control, versatility and tactics. With experience, she is gaining control and better command of the court. She took the 1998 inaugural women's Grand Slam Cup, showing increasing confidence. Will she be able to out-think Martina?

# Glossary of Tennis Terms

**ace** — a point scored by the server, when the opponent is unable to touch, or barely touches, the ball served. It flies past.

**backhand** — a stroke from the side of the body opposite the side the player normally serves from (left side for a right-handed server). Two-handed backhand means the player uses both hands to hold the racket and deliver the shot.

**baseliner** — a player who plays from the back of the court, near the baseline, usually using ground strokes to keep the ball in play. This is generally considered a steady, safer way to play tennis, but can still require power.

**court** — area on which tennis is played. A tennis court is 78 feet (23.77 metres) long and 36 feet (10.97 m) wide. The baseline is the back line of the court on both sides. The sideline for singles play and service is 4 1/2 feet (1.37 m) inside the doubles sideline. The court may be made of differing surfaces — among them hard (perhaps asphalt or concrete), clay, carpet or grass. The way the players move and the way the ball bounces in play varies according to the court surfaces. Some players tend to play better on one surface.

**crosscourt** — a shot that travels diagonally across the court.

**deuce** — a tie score in a game, where both players have 40 points (40–all). The first point taken after deuce is called advantage, either for the server ("advantage server") or the receiver ("advantage receiver"). At deuce, one of the players must get two points in a row to win. In the spectacular 1995 Wimbledon final, Arantxa Sanchez Vicario lost to Steffi Graf after 13 deuces.

**drop shot** — a shot aimed to just clear the net, and fall close to the net, when the opponent is playing near the baseline. Such a shot may win the point or force the opponent to race to the net.

**fault** — an infraction of the rules of play of tennis. A fault is called when a player's serve hits the net, or the ball served falls outside the opposite service court. If the server steps on the baseline, or misses hitting the ball during the serve, that too is a fault. If a server commits two faults in a row that is a double fault and she loses a point.

**game** — smallest division of a tennis match. The first player to win six games and be two games ahead wins the set. The points in a game are called love, 15, 30, 40, advantage, and game. The server's score is mentioned first, except in games that reach a tie. For example, when the server wins the first point in a game, the score is 15–0 (fifteen-love). When the server loses the first point, the score is 0–15 (love–fifteen). When ties occur, the score is 15–all, 30–all, or deuce (40–all).

**Grand Slam** — winning all of the four major championships in tennis: the Australian Open, French Open, Wimbledon, and US Open. Also a descriptive term for these events.

**ground stroke** — any shot a player uses to hit the ball back after the ball has bounced once on the court.

**International Tennis Federation (ITF)** — the world governing body of tennis, controlling most amateur matches and the major professional championships. About 100 countries belong to the ITF.

**lob** — a shot hit high in the air. It is intended to go over the head of the opponent.

**love** — the scoring word for zero points.

**majors** — the four most important championships in tennis each year: the Australian Open, French Open, Wimbledon, and US Open. Also known as the Big

Four. Sometimes these are called Grand Slam events, too. If a player wins all four in one calendar year, she has made a Grand Slam.

**match** — the overall tennis contest, including a number of sets.

**Open Era** — period begun in 1968 with the decision by the ITF to allow both amateur and professional tennis players to play in tournaments offering prize money. These tournaments are called "open". Now all important national title events are open.

**overhead smash** — a hard stroke swung at the ball from above the head, like a serve.

**rally** — a long period of exchanged strokes between players.

**seeding** — a ranking list of tennis players. The strongest players are seeded first, and so on. Tournaments are set up so that strong players do not play one another in the early rounds. This keeps the stars in the tournament longer.

**set** — a division of a tennis match consisting of a number of games. The first player to win at least six games, and be ahead of her opponent by two games, wins the set. Most tournaments now use tie breakers when the score becomes tied at six games all. The player who wins two out of three sets wins the match.

**straight sets** — two sets won in a row. When a player wins two sets in a row, she has won the match, since two out of three sets is a win. Winning in straight sets is often a short and decisive victory, showing the strength of the winner's game.

**tie breaker** — a play-off at six games all to prevent long, drawn-out matches. Before the introduction of the tie breaker, there was no limit to the number of games that could be played in a set. In a tie breaker a player must be the first to reach at least six points, and be ahead by two points, in order to win the set.

**volley** — any shot that hits the ball during play, before the ball has bounced on the court. Most volleys are made close to the net and are meant to be quick winners. The net player risks losing the point to a high lob that goes over her head and lands just inside the baseline.

**Women's Tennis Association (WTA)** — association formed in 1972 to represent professional women tennis players. It also supervises tournaments and ranks players according to the points they have earned.

# Research Sources

Adams, Deatrice C. "In Her Name."
http://www.dreamin.com/ausf.htm (08/24/98)

Bodo, Peter. "I'm doing pretty good for my age," *Tennis,* Vol. 32,
Issue 5, September 1996, p. 95-.
http://www.epnet.com/cgi-bin/epwnorb (08/24/98)

DiManno, Rosie. "Martina looks to double her fun," *The Toronto
Star,* August 24, 1998, p. C3.

Doherty, Donna. "Mother knows daughter best," *Tennis,* Vol. 33,
Issue 9, January, 1998, p. 34-. http://www.epnet.com/cgi-
bin/epwdag (08/24/98)

"Dreams answered: Davenport is No. 1," *The Toronto Star,*
October 10, 1998, p. E9.

Harwitt, Sandra. "Martina Defends First Grand Slam in Straight
Sets," Tennis Magazine Online, http://www.tennis-
magazine.com/slams/oz98/3la.htm (08/24/98)
————. "Martina II."
http://www.justwomen.com/feat_Martina.html (08/24/98)

Heilpern, John. "Born to Serve," *Vogue,* Vol. 187, July 1997, p. 160.

Higdon, David. "Beyond power," *Tennis,* Vol. 33, Issue 10,
February, 1998, p. 26-. http://www.epnet.com/cgi-
bin/epwdag (08/24/98)

Jenkins, Sally. "Proceed with Caution," *Sports Illustrated,* Vol. 81,
Issue 16, October 17, 1994, p. 22-.
http://www.epnet.com/cgi-bin/epwnorb (08/26/98)

Kennedy, Dana. "Blue Skies" *Sports Illustrated,*
http://www.cnnsi.com/features/1997/womenmag/bluesk
ies.html (08/20/98)

Leand, Andrea. "Repeat Performances," *Tennis,* Vol. 34, No. 5,
September 1998, p. 37.
————. "Stroke of Genius," *Sport,* June, 1998, p. 92.

Marachiello, Tony. "Heat is on Swiss Miss," *The Toronto Sun*, August 20, 1998, p. 112.

"Martina Navratilova on Martina," *Tennis*, Vol. 32, Issue 10, February, 1997, p. 27-. http://www.epnet.com/cgi-bin/epwnorb (08/26/98)

McKee Court Reporting, Inc. "Press Interview with Martina April 1, 1997." http://www.kmdmcr@aol.com (08/17/98)

Nando.net; Agence France-Presse, "Martina donates money to vaccination program," Geneva, October 16, 1997. http://www.sportserver.com/newsroom/spo...h/ten/feat/archive/101697/ten20038.html

Preston, Mark. "Court Chatter," *Tennis*, Vol. 34, Issue 1, May 1998, p. 15. http://www.epnet.com.cgi-bin/epwnorb (08/14/98)

Price, S. L. "Over the top," *Sports Illustrated*, Vol. 86, No. 14, April 7, 1997, p. 64.

Richardson, Kevin. "Aces," *Elle*, Issue 144, August 1997, p. 125. http://www.epnet.com/cgi-bin/epwtop (08/25/98)

Starr, Mark. "Martina Redux," *Newsweek*, Vol. 129, June 2, 1997, p. 61.

Tebbutt, Tom. "Martina cruises to victory," *Globe and Mail*, September 1, 1998, p. S2.

Teitelbaum, Michael. Grand Slam Stars (New York: HarperCollins, 1998), p. 15.

"The teen queens," *Newsweek*, Vol. 132, Issue 8, August 24, 1998, p. 48. http://www.epnet.com/cgi-bin/epwtop (08/25/98)

Wescott, Gail Cameron, Helga Chudacoff-Lonne, et al. "Sweet Sixteen," *People*, Vol. 47, Issue 24, June 23, 1997, p. 83. http://www.epnet.com/cgi-bin/epwtop (08/25/98)

Wright, Lisa. "Cool Martina stops Seles to reach Open semifinals," *The Toronto Star*, September 9, 1998, p. C8.